SUNSHINE
for the
COURAGEOUS
LATTER-DAY
SAINT
SOUL

SUNSHINE

for the

COURAGEOUS
LATTER-DAY
SAINT
SOUL

EAGLE GATE

SALT LAKE CITY, UTAH

We acknowledge copyright holders whose stories or poems we may have included but with whom we were unable to make personal contact. Other works are in public domain. If any acknowledgments have been overlooked, please notify the publisher and omissions will be rectified in future editions.

Library of Congress Cataloging-in-Publication Data

Sunshine for the courageous Latter-day Saint soul.
    p.   cm.
    ISBN 1-57345-900-3 (pbk.)
    1. Christian life—Mormon authors.   I. Eagle Gate.
BX8656 .S86 2001
248.4'893—dc21

2001004015

Printed in the United States of America   54459-6778

Malloy Lithographing Incorporated, Ann Arbor, Michigan

10 9 8 7 6 5 4 3 2 1

Contents

Walking by Faith, I Am Blessed Every Hour

Do What Is Right

But a Small Moment

The Integrity of the Heart

Fresh Courage Take . . . All Is Well

God Our Strength Will Be

The Spirit Is Willing

Thy Soldiers: Faithful, True, and Bold

The Youth of Zion

Preface

"And they were all young men, and they were exceedingly valiant for courage, and also for strength and activity; but behold, this was not all—they were men who were true at all times in whatsoever thing they were entrusted.

"Yea, they were men of truth and soberness, for they had been taught to keep the commandments of God and to walk uprightly before him. . . .

"And now I say unto you, my beloved brother Moroni, that never had I seen so great courage, nay, not amongst all the Nephites.

"For as I had ever called them my sons (for they were all of them very young) even so they said unto me: Father, behold our God is with us, and he will not suffer that we should fall; then let us go forth; we would not slay our brethren if they would let us alone; therefore let us go. . . .

"Now they never had fought, yet they did not fear death; and they did think more upon the liberty of their fathers than they did upon their lives" (Alma 53: 20–21; 56: 45–47).

Never before had the great prophet and warrior Helaman seen such courage in his men—not until he was chosen to lead the two thousand stripling warriors into battle to defend their covenants and their faith.

Indeed, it is faith that most often calls forth such extraordinary courage. It is faith that pulls the wounded and weary through the battles of war, spirit, and health. It is faith that makes courage possible, turning hope into diligence and fear into prayers.

Sunshine for the Courageous Latter-day Saint Soul is a collection of 101 stories about those who have been faithful and courageous, those who have overcome defeat and sorrow to find that peace is the reward of endurance.

With selections from such beloved authors as Linda J. Eyre, Ardeth G. Kapp, David O. McKay, John A. Widtsoe, Hugh B. Brown, Janice Kapp Perry, and Spencer W. Kimball, this collection addresses courage on ten fronts:

"Be Strong and of Good Courage," which includes stories about valor in everyday situations at home, work, or school.

"Walking by Faith, I Am Blessed Every Hour," a section that features the stories of those whose courage comes from keeping their faith.

"Do What Is Right," which includes accounts of those who have used moral courage to stand up for their beliefs.

"But a Small Moment," which is full of experiences that have come as a result of suffering and adversity.

"The Integrity of the Heart," a section comprised of touching stories about testimony and valiance.

"Fresh Courage Take . . . All Is Well," which highlights the faith and courage of the pioneers.

"God Our Strength Will Be," a section devoted to stories about courage in the mission field.

"The Spirit Is Willing," an uplifting section about courage in battling physical ailments.

"Thy Soldiers: Faithful, True, and Bold," which addresses courage on the battlefield.

"The Youth of Zion," which is full of stories about courageous teenagers of noble birthright.

The publisher thanks the many authors whose stories are included in this volume, as well as Marilynne Linford, who wrote and collected more than a dozen of the stories included here; Lisa Mangum, who compiled the bulk of the stories and did preliminary editing; and Lindsay McAllister, who helped pare down a huge collection of stories to the 101 now included.

Be Strong
and of
Good Courage

"Let Me Be Brave in the Attempt"

JACK R. CHRISTIANSON

$\mathscr{S}$ome years ago my wife and I took our children to a Special Olympics track meet. . . . We knew that the Special Olympians were people with great spirits who had outward mental or physical handicaps, yet who, despite their limitations, were real people with real feelings and real needs. Though none of these athletes would ever be famous or go down as champions in the world's record books, they were champions because they were doing their best.

We wanted to teach our children this vital lesson about life. We wanted them to know that the motto for Special Olympics was not just for Special Olympians, but it applied to everyday life as well: "Let me win. But if I cannot win, let me be brave in the attempt." We may not always be the very best or always win, but we can always be brave. . . .

The track meet proved to be the teacher we hoped it would be. Our children loved the events as they got used to the open shows of affection and the athletes' mannerisms. They watched the "huggers" hug every participant after each event. They felt the love and warmth of athletes and volunteers. However, the most significant lesson came with the women's one-hundred-meter dash.

One of the participants was a woman in her twenties with Down's syndrome. She was big-boned and heavyset—not what you would think of as a sprinter. We noticed that she had split her pant seam and had used a large safety pin to fasten the front of her pants; yet it appeared to be a futile attempt.

When the starting gun was fired, the runners took off. The woman with the safety pin was dead last. It was difficult for her to run, but she did the best she could. Then it happened. The safety pin popped, her pants fell to her ankles, and she ran two more difficult steps before falling flat on her face.

I wanted to jump from the stands and help her. Before I could move, however, she stood up, pulled up her pants, held them together in front with one hand, and hobbled to the end of the race. When she crossed the finish line she fell into the outstretched arms of a hugger. Everyone cheered for her as if she had won the race. Tears welled up in my eyes as I witnessed her courage. I knew that if that had happened to me I would have found a place to hide rather than finish the race.

The story does not end there, however. When the medals were awarded, she stood on the platform still holding her pants together with one hand. When they presented her with a medal, she bent over so they could place it around her neck. As she stood up, the excitement of having a medal was evidently too much for her to bear. She raised both arms above her head in triumph to wave excitedly to the crowd, forgetting her pants predicament. Her pants fell to her ankles again. But she didn't seem to mind that she stood before the large crowd in her underwear. The important thing was that she had done her best. She had been brave, and that was what really counted.

I hope I never forget the feelings of that day. I knew I had watched a true champion—one who did the best she could even though she wasn't the winner.

Motherhood:
The Greatest Career

LINDA J. EYRE

In New York City in 1982, at a meeting of the National Council of Women, probably the oldest and most recognized women's organization in America, I heard a young woman, Elizabeth Nichols, author of *The Coming Matriarchy,* speak to a large group of prestigious women. She suggested that the future family would be "rotational," meaning that not only mothers and fathers but also children would rotate from unit to unit until they found satisfactory settings for particular times in their lives. She said that food preparation would be referred to as almost a thing of the past because of all the modern computerized conveniences; thus, a woman could spend much more time working outside the home. "When the woman is granted equal financial rewards for her work," she said, "then she will have her own financial base and at last she will be able to marry for love instead of money."

I stirred uneasily in my seat and looked around to see if I could read the faces in the room. *Do they really believe that?* I thought as I saw a few nods, a few raised eyebrows, but mostly inscrutable stares.

Growing more and more apprehensive as time went on, I heard other speakers say such things as, "The greatest need in America today is for quality, twenty-four-hour-a-day child-care centers so that mothers can be free to work day or night." I began to wonder if our society was working to live or living to work.

The theme of the conference was "Women and Work: Families and the Future." But so much was being said about women and work, and so little about real families. I was anxious, partly because that very afternoon, in front of this same noble body of women, I was to give a two-minute response to a special citation I had been selected to receive. I was one of six women under the age of thirty-five who was being cited for outstanding achievement in their careers. The careers of the other five recipients spanned from treasurer of the United States to publisher of *Harper's Magazine.* My award, as nearly as I could tell, was being given for my bearing and teaching children and for furthering the cause of families.

The statement I was going to make, which Richard and I had carefully worked out just a few hours before, was the exact opposite of what had been said up to that point.

That afternoon, at the moment my name was called, I was terrified. I believed what I had to say; however, and say it I would. As I stood listening to the person reading my citation, I took heart a bit when she came to the part that said, "She is the mother of seven children." An audible gasp and a buzz went through the audience that prevented the reader momentarily from continuing. I saw many smiles and several looks that seemed to say, "You must be from Mars." Still, I could not tell if the smiles were of amusement or encouragement, and when the reader had finished and I had received the citation from Governor Cary of New York, I stepped to the podium and [concluded my speech with] the following:

"You know, all of us here, whether conscious of it or not, have multiple careers. We are all involved in more than one thing. In some careers the bottom line is profit. In others it is productivity. Those of us who write have a bottom line of publication, and in the arts we like to think we aim at perfection. In teaching, the bottom line is pupils and preparedness. But there is another career, and I think it is the most demanding and multi-faceted career of all, in which the bottom line is people—little people—our children.

"We have embarked, my husband and I, over the last few years, on an effort to popularize parenting. Our work at the White House, our writing, and our national network of parents' groups have aimed at helping people realize that our most significant and serious problems, both personal and societal, have their roots in our homes, and that parenting, when it is pursued seriously and thoughtfully, is not only life's most important career, but its most joyful and fulfilling career. Thank you."

The response was overwhelming. The audience came alive. Their enthusiastic applause told me that they had believed what I said, or at least had wanted to believe it.

I suddenly realized that this audience was not hostile. Most of them were mothers who secretly wished that someone would validate their role and say something positive about families. Most knew that mothering is a career—the hardest and the best!

In a reception line afterward many clamored over our two oldest children, who were with us, and warmly and sincerely congratulated me. I felt that, through me, they were congratulating all . . . dedicated mothers who have devoted [their] lives to a career at home rearing a family, regardless of whatever other career [they] may have.

The Missing Shoe

MARVIN J. ASHTON

*M*any years ago I witnessed a state championship high school track meet at Brigham Young University. A lesson I learned as I watched the mile run was most impressive. I know I shall never forget it.

About a dozen young men had qualified to represent their schools. The starting gun was fired, and these young men who had trained so long and so hard took off. Four of them, closely bunched together, took the early lead. Suddenly the runner in second place spiked the first runner's foot with his shoe. As the leader was about to make the next stride forward, he found that he was without a shoe.

Seeing this, I wondered what the leader would do because of what his competitor had unintentionally done to him. It seemed to me he had a number of choices. He could take a few extra quick sprints and catch up to the fellow who had put him out of first position, double up his fist, and hit him to get even. He could run over to the coach and say, "This is what you get. I've trained all my life for this big day, and now look what's happened!" He could run off into the stands and say to his mother, father, or girlfriend, "Isn't this horrible?", or he could have sat down on the track and cried. But he did none of these things. He just kept running.

He was halfway around the first lap, and I thought to myself, "Good for him. He'll finish this first lap of the four and retire gracefully." But after he completed the first lap, he just kept running. He completed the second lap, then the third lap—and every time he took a stride, cinders were coming up through his stocking, hurting his foot. (They ran on cinder tracks in those days.) But he didn't quit. He just kept running.

I thought, "What an outstanding display of courage and self-discipline! What parents! What a coach! What leaders who have affected his life enough so that in a situation like this he would not stop running!" He finished the job he had to do. He did not place first, but he was a real winner. When I walked over to him at the completion of the race and congratulated him on his courageous performance, he was composed and in complete control. He was able to carry on when it would have been much easier to quit.

I Wish You Could Know That Kind of Joy

KATHLEEN H. BARNES

One day while I was standing on a Salt Lake City street, a woman approached me, asked a couple of questions, and then launched a verbal attack, beginning with her opinion that Mormon women are brainwashed and subservient. She accused us of coercing our children and stripping them of their abilities to make independent decisions. (She obviously didn't know some of our children.) She claimed we forced others to our way of thinking. She implied that Mormon women were illiterate and mindless. She had clearly formed a judgment against Latter-day Saint women so comprehensive, angry, and misinformed that I knew I could not turn it around. Frankly, I didn't dare try because she was a hefty woman, much larger than I am, and I was certain that if I provoked a blow, I would soon find myself a blob on the sidewalk.

So I listened and let her unload. After what seemed like endless minutes of ugly verbiage, she appeared satisfied that she had sufficiently impacted me with her message, and she fell silent, glaring at me, waiting for me to respond. We speak of fear; but I can tell you that I knew fear at that moment. I felt physically threatened as well as wounded by her words.

I began to respond, saying the only thing that came into my mind. "Someday," I said, "you may open your door to some young Latter-day Saint missionaries. Before you slam it, please remember that somewhere they have a mother just like you and just like me, who is praying for them and for those they meet. Then you might want to say, 'I met a Mormon woman once, and she told me that she was the happiest person alive. She said her happiness did not come from riches or fame. Her happiness was rooted deeply in her heart and came from a rich understanding of life and her connection to her Savior. She said she lived with a kind of joy and peace that comes from God. She said she wished that I, too, could know that kind of joy.' And then at that point, if you want to, you can tell those young missionaries, 'Thank you, but I am not interested in your message.'" To my surprise, the woman hung her head for a moment, muttered, "Thanks," then turned and walked away.

That day I learned that a simple expression of feelings can often diffuse an attack. So when all else fails, just speak from your heart. We need not be timid, nor do we need to defend ourselves. . . .

For the most part, Latter-day Saint women do not lack in belief, but sometimes we lack the confidence to express our beliefs in forthright but accepting ways. Our convictions will not always be echoed in others, of course, but they will generally be met with respect if stated with confidence and simple honesty.

Courage

GRANTLAND RICE

I'd like to think that I can look at
　death and smile and say,
All I have left now is my final breath,
　take that away
And you must either leave me dust or
　dreams or in far flight
The soul that wanders where the star-
　dust streams through endless night.

I'd rather think that I can look at life
　with this to say,
Send what you will of struggle or of
　strife, blue skies or gray,
I'll stand against the final charge of hate
　by peak and pit
And nothing in the steel clad fist of fate
　can make me quit.

Seeking the Will of God: Bit by Bit by Bit

PAM KAZMAIER

*W*hen I was asked to [speak at Women's Conference on my experiences in] seeking God's will in decision making, I was sure I should say no. I had just been watching the news on CNN, and interest rates and the stock market were falling. My husband and I had prayerfully invested five thousand dollars in the stock that was plummeting. Obviously, I'm not a good decision maker, I thought. I was waiting for an opening in the conversation so I could say no. Then my knees started shaking just as they do before I bear my testimony on fast Sunday at church. I felt I was supposed to say yes—that I was supposed to tell of my recent experience in making the hardest decision of my life: I quit my career as a nurse to stay at home with my two small children.

. . . [Understand that] I'm not advocating that all women should quit their jobs to stay home with their children—especially after having done it for two years. I thought I worked hard as a nurse—but being a mother is the hardest thing I've ever done.

Let me explain why this decision was so difficult. I grew up in Illinois. I was completely ignorant about Latter-day Saints. I thought they all wore black and lived in the Rocky Mountains. I was reared by a mother who was a feminist back in the fifties before that term was coined. She reared my two sisters and me not to marry or have children but to get an education and have a career. My father did not disagree.

At the age of eighteen, I entered a convent, largely because I didn't want to worry about being married and having children. I valued my mother's teachings and was afraid that if I went to college, I'd fall in love, get married, and have children. A convent seemed a good place to avoid all that.

The scriptures are another strong reason I entered the convent; they are also the reason I left. The longer I was in the convent, the more I read the scriptures and prayed, the more I felt the Holy Spirit tell me that I was in the wrong place. I didn't understand that then. I do now. I *was* in the wrong place there; I was supposed to be here.

So even though being a nun was a wonderful part of my life, after four years I left the convent. Making that decision was very tough. . . . While I was a nun, I began nurse's training in earnest. . . . I loved the nursing profession and thought I would never leave it. I started at fourteen as a candy striper and completed my training in 1977 after I had left the convent.

I was not like young Latter-day Saint women who are

taught eternal values early and are groomed to marry in the temple and be wives and mothers. Those were all foreign ideas to me. But at twenty-eight I did marry. Like me, my husband, Kevin, supported the idea of women working and believed they should be independent. At the time of our marriage, Kevin and I decided not to have children because they'd get in the way of our work. His career came first; my career came first. It was a great match. . . .

I loved everything about the hospital—the smell, the excitement. It was just a great place; it felt like home. I joined the Church because of people I met there. I found myself taking care of patients who were different from anybody I had ever met. They were amazing; I wanted to be like them. These patients had something I didn't have—peace. I was attracted to their strength in crisis, their family unity. They were mannerly and polite, well-groomed and refined. To me, my conversion experience was a miracle. I joined the Church in Mesa, Arizona, and my life changed.

My patriarchal blessing said, "There are spirits reserved in the heavens so that you and your husband can have children." I thought, *Yeah, right. These Mormons have all these children. Not me.* Then, a year and a half later, my husband joined the Church, and his patriarchal blessing said, "There are *still* spirits reserved in heaven so that you and your wife can have children." "Oh, Kevin," I said, "I think we've got to have these children. Oh no." And so we did. We sold our Corvette and bought a family car. . . .

At thirty-five I had my first little boy, and then at thirty-seven I had another.

I still never considered quitting work, though. I thought having the children was going to be enough. Then I had a run-in with a little pink pamphlet—*Mothers in Zion.* I hear it made quite a stir in the Church when it came out, but it didn't faze me because I didn't have any children then. When I first saw it, I thought, *Oh yeah, right, uh-huh, very good,* and I shelved it. It wasn't about me. But then one day my husband said, seeing me wrestle with motherhood and work, "Maybe you ought to think about quitting work." Ha! Quit work? He could just as well have said, "Maybe you ought to cut off your legs." I loved my job—and I was very good at it. I couldn't cook. I couldn't sew. I can't sing. I can't do anything. But give me a chest pain, and I know what to do.

I told my husband I would pray about quitting work, fully thinking the Lord would say, "Of course you can't quit your job. It's a vocation; it's a calling. You and I have done this for twenty years. You can't quit. People are waiting for you in the hospital." So I just prayed, "Okay, Lord, this is what Kevin thinks, but you and I both know . . ." and then on like that. I got up from my knees and never thought another thing about it. . . .

The next day, this pink pamphlet that had been shelved for four years was hanging out of my bookshelves. My husband doesn't get up in my bookshelves. My kids were too little. And I hadn't been in that section—that was the dusty section. But the pink pamphlet was hanging out. That's a miracle. How did that happen? I had ten minutes before I left for work—I was never late for work—so I thought, *Okay, I've got ten minutes to read this thing. There is something in here about mothers working.* (That's how much attention I had paid to it when I first got it.) I thought, *I'm going to read something in here that will prove to Kevin that I should keep on working.* So I started reading the pamphlet, and before I knew it I was crying. I read, "No more sacred word exists in secular or holy writ than that of *mother.* There is no more noble work than that of a good and God-fearing mother." It went on and on—"a mother's role is God-ordained" (Ezra Taft Benson, "To the Mothers in Zion," Parents Fireside, Salt Lake City, Utah, 22 February 1987). *Oh, brother!* I thought. *I'm sunk.* I cried all the way to work.

I had great baby-sitters. My kids were in better hands with them than they were with me. The sitters had play dough and children's tapes and other kids running around, and everybody was happy. I left our children with the baby-sitter on the way to work and said, "Yes! I'm out of here. I'm going someplace where I know what I'm doing." But this day I drove to work sobbing.

I'm not like Abraham, who could immediately sacrifice Isaac the very next morning. I couldn't tell my head nurse, "I read this article and . . ." It took weeks and weeks, months and months. It was a very gradual change for me. I got home that night and thought, *Sure, women are supposed to leave working at McDonald's and the dry cleaners, but I have this important calling of the Lord to be a nurse.* So I checked in with the pamphlet again, only to read, "Finally President Kimball counsels,

'I beg of you, you who could and should be bearing and rearing a family: wives come home from the typewriter, the laundry, *the nursing*'" (emphasis added). I was devastated, shattered.

I began to pray with real intent this time. For months I prayed about it. I was on my knees to the Lord saying, "Lord, how can you expect me to give up something I am so good at to do something I am so bad at?" It didn't make any sense to me. And I heard the voice of the Lord: "I am just asking you to do something *else* now." I was speechless. I knew it was the voice of the Lord. It was that still, small voice I had read about in the scriptures. I thought, *Oh, he wants me to do something* else *now. It isn't like he didn't appreciate all those years of service. He's asking me to do something* else *now. . . .*

I was so glad he let me wean myself from full time, to part time, to on call. That is how my testimony has grown—bit by bit by bit.

The final step came for me one night when I came home after only four hours at the hospital. I drove into my driveway and saw my husband, my dear husband whom I love, outside speaking to our next-door neighbor. It was dark and cold. It gets that way in Arizona in the evenings even though it's hot during the days. There were my two little boys, barefoot and dirty. In wet T-shirts with their hair all caked, they looked like orphans. *I just left four hours ago,* I thought. *How can they look this bad already?* When I'm home I line those kids up just like my IV fluids. I organize them, and they are in bed and asleep by eight o'clock. They would have had their little jammies on and their baths and their prayers and their stories and their teethies brushed and everything.

It was not the moment to discuss with Kevin the differences in our parenting styles. So I went into the house, put down my stethoscope, rolled up my sleeves, and tore into the disaster area that used to be the kitchen. And I once again heard the calm voice, not my own, say in my mind, "There are others who can take your place at work, but there is no one who can take your place here." And I said, "No kidding!" Just like that. Out loud. I wasn't feeling at all spiritual at the time, so when I heard the voice of the Lord, I just said, "No kidding! No kidding."

As I said, I am no Abraham. Months had gone by since I had begun praying about work. It wasn't until the next week that I woke up one morning with the thought, I'm going to quit my job today. I need to tell Kevin. . . . He didn't know that I'd been brooding about work for months and months.

Kevin was my last hurdle. He really liked my salary, really liked the fact that I was working. If there was some way I could convince him. . . . I was on my knees in prayer right there by the bathtub after he left, praying, "Heavenly Father, I've got to quit today, and I don't know how to do it. I don't know how I'm going to tell Kevin, and you've got to help me."

When Kevin came home, I was sobbing. I felt like somebody had died. Kevin came in and said, "The Holy Spirit told me on the way home in the truck. You're going to quit your job today." I was so grateful to

Heavenly Father for hearing my prayer so I didn't have to tell Kevin. . . .

"How do I do this?" I asked. "I've never quit a job. I've been there at this hospital for eleven years. I love nursing. Over twenty years I've been a nurse. I don't know how to do this."

"Well, you need to go tell your head nurse."

"Yeah. Go tell the head nurse. Okay." So we got in the car and drove to the hospital. I sobbed all the way up the stairs to the sixth floor. . . . Thank goodness my head nurse was in her office. I blurted out, "Sally, I've got to quit my job." And then she was crying and I was crying, and it was awful, just awful. But I did it. That was two years ago this week, and I am still alive. . . .

And I know I am doing the right thing now, too. . . .

In Matthew 6:33, the Savior instructs: "Seek ye first the kingdom of God, and his righteousness; and all these things shall be added unto you." If he had not said "first," wouldn't that be easier? Wouldn't it be great if he'd said, "Seek ye *third* the kingdom of God"? Wouldn't that be a lot more convenient? But he says, "Seek ye *first* the kingdom of God." Seeking the kingdom of God first is *hard.* Usually I find I have to sacrifice something of the world to do it. Right now, that means putting my ambitions aside for my children.

Old Temple Shoes

DAVID C. GAUNT

I was serving in the Jordan River Utah Temple as a supervisor when I asked Brother Robins, a new temple worker who had just completed his training, to officiate at an endowment session that day. He was nervous and stammered a few things about how it would be his first time and he didn't feel ready. I remembered how I felt my first time officiating on a session and could sympathize with his uncertainty. I reassured him that I had noticed his dedication, his study, and his personal preparation as an ordinance worker, and promised him that he would be able to officiate in his holy office without any problems. He agreed, though I suspected he was still nervous.

Later in the day, as the time for the endowment session neared, I saw Brother Robins come in. There was a mixture of humility, honor, and hesitation in his bearing. He was dressed immaculately all in white. His clothes had been carefully pressed and cleaned, except for his shoes. They were old and faded and cracked. As he walked toward me, I noticed that they didn't quite fit him. I wondered if, in his nervousness, Brother Robins had accidentally slipped on someone else's shoes.

We exchanged pleasantries, and then Brother Robins said, "I noticed you were looking at my shoes." He looked down at his well-worn shoes, the laces carefully knotted. "Well, you see, my father served as a temple worker in the Manti Utah Temple before he died. I was feeling so afraid, I thought if I wore my father's shoes, I would have the courage to officiate."

Tears filled my eyes as I watched this humble brother officiate flawlessly an endowment session in the holy temple—standing tall and confident in his father's old temple shoes.

Lessons Learned
from Uncle Teddy

LOWELL L. BENNION

When I was fourteen years of age and my brother sixteen, we went to work on a ranch 180 miles from home, driving all day in a chain-driven truck to get there.

Uncle Teddy was our employer, a man who had as much courage in adversity as any man I have ever known. He had a way with boys. Seldom did he give detailed instructions; he simply told us what to do and expected us to do it. The first time we harnessed a team of horses, we put on the collars upside down. One day we were told to clear off ten acres of sagebrush. We had never done anything like this before and were making slow progress. So I went to find Uncle Teddy to get him to tell us how to do it. His answer was simply that a neighbor boy, whom we had thought quite stupid, had grubbed out ten acres the previous spring and done a fine job. Nothing more needed to be said; we cleared the field of brush.

Before the summer was over, we had changed the

course of a mountain creek, dug a new canal, put in miles of fencing, and helped put up a stack or two of hay every day for weeks. But best of all, we had come to feel strength in our shoulders, backs, arms, and legs. More thrilling than our physical strength, however, was the self-confidence we had gained. No longer were we afraid of tackling any new job.

After working for Uncle Teddy for two summers, I was afraid of no man. I suppose if the Lord had asked me to run the universe, I would have answered, "Yes sir, when shall I begin," so great was the strength, courage, self-confidence, and independence of spirit that I had gained.

"Are You Having a Bad Day?"

MARY ELLEN EDMUNDS

*L*ove requires courage. To share in Christ's way is a courageous undertaking. Do it. Do it now. Respond to promptings that come.

We must not ever ignore an impulse to serve when there's something we could do. When it's within our power to give love, we should never withhold it. If we feel compassion or empathy without doing something, we may diminish our power to act, to respond.

I find that I *think* of kind things more often than I *do* kind things. I'll get an idea, a prompting, but then too many times I chicken out. When I *do* respond, I have great adventures.

Once I was in a store standing in line to check out. (I have lots of experiences with that particular activity, and I almost always get in the slowest line; I don't know if it's a gift or a talent.) Anyway, I noticed that the woman behind the checkout counter seemed to be in a less-than-pleasant mood. She kind of locked horns with a person ahead of me in line. I couldn't really hear or tell exactly what happened, but the clerk was not happy. A little prompting came inside of me: "Say something nice to her." "I don't want to." "She needs it." (Do you ever have conversations like this with the still small voice?) "She'll bite my head off." Back and forth it went. I was getting closer. My heart was pounding the way it does when you sit in a testimony meeting and you know you're going to get up, and you also know you're going to die at the pulpit.

And then I was there, right up close to her. She was punching the keys and all. And this is what came out of my mouth: "Are you having a bad day?" It came out kindly and gently and seemed to catch her way off guard. She looked at me, getting ready to bite, and then said, "Does it show?" "Kind of." She then told me that yes, she was having a very hard, bad, ugly day, and she told me some of the reasons why.

I didn't know what to do. I was screaming at the still small voice in my mind, *"Now* what? You didn't tell me what to do next!" But it came out: "Can I do anything to help you?" She looked at me with this what-in-the-world kind of look. It was an awkward moment. Then I said, "I know how to take out the trash." And we both laughed.

We continued talking to each other as she finished ringing up my purchases. She thanked me as I left, and I felt so happy that I was grinning—not just smiling, but grinning. I felt good all over. I'm not sure if that little exchange did much for the woman at the checkout, but it made a huge difference in my day and is a sweet memory even now, years later.

Standing for Standards

RANDALL C. BIRD

*R*ich had been voted the A-2 player of the year in Idaho. He stood about 6'4" tall and weighed about 220 pounds. The guy was built—his body looked like an upside-down pyramid. The girls all thought he was handsome, but his physical traits aren't what impressed me. He was tough spiritually.

At one time in his school, it was popular to throw the girls into the boys' locker room in the hopes of embarrassing them. One day Rich happened to be in the dressing room when this happened. As the girl was thrown screaming into the locker room, Rich, who was totally dressed, left. He walked toward a group of young men who were laughing at the incident. Rich asked if any of them had thrown the girl in, and one young man responded, "Yes, I did." Rich grabbed the young man by the shirt, lifted him up against the wall, and asked, "Did you think it was funny?"

Meanwhile, the girl had left the locker room and was watching from a distance. The boy hanging from Rich's hand shook his head until his cheeks flapped and, with fear in his voice, he replied, "No, no."

Then Rich said something that perhaps was not very Christian. He said, "If you ever do that again, I'll break your face!" Then he put the boy back down.

Now here is an important question: Do you think Rich became any less popular because he refused to go along with something he felt was wrong, even though it was considered the popular thing to do? Of course he didn't. In fact, you can probably imagine what was going through the mind of the girl who watched from a distance. You can almost hear her thinking, "Oh, what a man!"

Rich's spiritual strength didn't stop with this incident. Once Rich was playing in a key football game between the first and second teams in the state. Following a sound defeat (the score was 41–6), this young man stepped onto the bus to find members of his team swearing and being downright crude. Rich stood up and said, "Now, we got beat, but we're not that kind of a team, so knock it off." Silence replaced vulgarity. What an example he was to the rest of the team.

You may be thinking, "Sure, he can get away with that. After all, he was 6'4" and weighed 220 pounds. What if he'd have been 5'4" and weighed 110?" Actually, I don't think that would have mattered much to Rich. I can almost picture him standing with his tiny frame and yelling in his high-pitched voice, "Now you guys sit down or I'll hit you in the knee."

You see, it wasn't Rich's size, or his good looks, or his athletic abilities that made him what he was. There are plenty of big, good-looking athletes who don't have the spiritual strength to stand up for what is right. It took courage for Rich to live up to his standards just as it does for someone who isn't quite as physically gifted. Standards should always remain the same regardless of a person's size.

Walking by Faith, I Am Blessed Every Hour

Priceless Faith

HUGH B. BROWN

$\mathcal{I}$ should like to introduce a story coming out of the first world war. I had a companion, a fellow officer, who was a very rich man, highly educated. He was a lawyer, had great power, was self-sufficient, and he said to me as we often talked of religion (because he knew who I was), "There is nothing in life that I would like to have that I cannot buy with my money."

Shortly thereafter he and I with two other officers were assigned to go to the city of Arras, France, which was under siege. It had been evacuated, and upon arrival there we thought there was no one in the city. We noted that the fire of the enemy was concentrated on the cathedral. We made our way to that cathedral and went in. There we found a little woman kneeling at an altar. We paused, respecting her devotion. Then shortly she arose, wrapped her little shawl around her frail shoulders, and came tottering down the aisle. The man among us who could speak better French said, "Are you in trouble?"

She straightened her shoulders, pulled in her chin,

and said, "No, I'm not in trouble. I was in trouble when I came here, but I've left it there at the altar."

"And what was your trouble?"

She said, "I received word this morning that my fifth son has given his life for France. Their father went first, and then one by one all of them have gone. But," straightening again, "I have no trouble; I've left it there because I believe in the immortality of the soul. I believe that men will live after death. I know that I shall meet my loved ones again."

When the little soul went out, there were tears in the eyes of the men who were there, and the one who had said to me that he could purchase anything with money turned to me and said, "You and I have seen men in battle display courage and valor that is admirable, but in all my life I have never seen anything to compare with the faith, the fortitude, and the courage of that little woman."

Then he said, "I would give all the money I have if I could have something of what she has."

Singing in the Choir

JANICE KAPP PERRY

*A*fter my first album of songs was recorded, I
started receiving requests to speak. I was fearful. . . . I
didn't know how to stand up and talk about my music.
[My husband], Doug, assured me that any woman in the
Church can stand up and bear her testimony about what
she personally has learned. But for at least two years, I
let my fears hold me back. Eventually I risked it. And it
was truly scary, start to finish. So I had to decide
whether to keep doing it and overcome my fear or just
quit trying. I kept trying. It took five years for me to
overcome my fear of speaking. And I still wouldn't *sing*
in public. Then a wise Hawaiian woman chastised me
when I declined to sing a solo at a Church meeting.
Holding back was a sign of pride. Just stand up, do your
best, and look to the Lord for your approval, not the
world, she instructed me. So I took her advice, and I've
been singing ever since and overcoming that fear.

For a time I was happy, contentedly doing everything that I loved. Then one day I read a brief article in
a doctor's office called "Feeling the Fear but Doing It

Anyway." Challenge yourself, the article suggested, to do something way beyond your abilities and see how far you get. Any little distance you cover will be a victory, and you might even make it! I told Doug about the article, and he suggested that I try out for the Tabernacle Choir. I nearly fell off my chair. That *was* out of reach—something I'd never even considered. But I asked around and learned that try-outs included three parts. First is a written test. I did that and passed. Then they require a home demo tape. So I did that and was told I passed. Next they would call me for a personal audition when there was an opening. After waiting two and a half years, I wrote in my journal, "I tried out for the Tabernacle Choir. I made it two-thirds of the way, and that was a victory." And I closed that chapter.

Several weeks later, I received a call inviting me to a personal audition. Talk about fear. "You'll always wonder if you don't try," Doug said. I was fifty-five. Choir members generally aren't accepted after age fifty-five because members have to retire at sixty. Doug went with me to audition. The person before me had the most exquisite, well-trained voice. I said, "Douglas, let's go before she comes out because I cannot do this." The door opened, Doug took my hand and pulled me into the audition room. I had never known fear like that. As I sang my audition, I thought, *Whose voice is this anyway? It's not mine.* I knew I had not done my best.

Afterwards I cried, certain that I would never sing in the Tabernacle Choir. Two weeks later, to my amazement, I received a call to sing in the choir. Sister JoAnn Ottley works with new choir members who may need a little extra vocal help. She called me in right away. I said, "Sister Ottley, when I auditioned, I was too afraid even to do what I can do. For my peace of mind, tell me, how did I get in the choir?" She answered, "Well, we could tell you were afraid. We knew your musical background from your written test, and we had heard your tape. But sometimes we hear a voice that won't *hurt* the choir, and we feel we can bring you along with us . . ." She paused a moment and then smiled, "The bottom line is we pray over every person who auditions, and if the Lord says yes, you're called. So work hard and be at peace."

I've now had five beautiful years in the choir that I wouldn't have had if I had listened to my fear. I'm almost sixty. Soon I'll have to quit, but I'll have been on a wonderful European tour first. If my fear had held me back from the audition, I would have missed it all. So don't let your fears hold you back.

The Ultimate Commitment

BYRON A. RASMUSSEN

I arrived in the Denmark Mission in November 1956. My first assignment was in the city of Aabenraa, with Elder Vaughn Rasmussen from Salt Lake City as my companion. We met with an investigator by the name of Holger Ravn for several weeks. Not knowing the language very well, I could not tell how he was receiving the gospel, but there was a good spirit in our meetings.

When Elder Rasmussen was assigned as district leader in Copenhagen, I received a new senior companion, Elder Cal Juel Andreasen from La Canada, California. After a few meetings, Mr. Ravn made a commitment to be baptized. I did not learn the story that follows until a couple more months passed and I was able to understand the language better.

After each meeting with Mr. Ravn, Elder Andreasen would fill me in on the discussion on the way home to our apartment. Since it was a long way home by bike, we talked a lot about Mr. Ravn. My companion told me that he had a testimony but was afraid of the persecution

40

that would follow baptism. He had a good job, but he was afraid his employer would fire him because he didn't want any Mormons working for him.

Finally my companion committed Mr. Ravn to baptism, and we made the arrangements for his baptism a week later. We had to travel from Aabenraa to Espjerg, where there was a baptismal font, and before we left to catch the bus, Mr. Ravn asked us to administer to him. After a long bus ride we arrived at Espjerg and went straight to the church, only to find it locked tight. After looking all over for the district leader with no success, we returned to Aabenraa without baptizing Mr. Ravn.

It was some time until Mr. Ravn would even talk to us, but finally, with patience, long-suffering, and love unfeigned, we were able to recommit him to baptism. When the arrangements were made this time, there was no possible way they could go awry. We had the district president and branch president follow up.

When we arrived, all was in readiness and a beautiful service was held. As I walked down into the waters of baptism with Mr. Ravn, he gripped my hand tightly and his breath was coming in short gasps. I turned him around and assumed the proper position, said the prayer, and baptized him. He came up gasping for air. He said, "Elder Rasmussen, why did you hold me under so long?" I explained that he had not been under the water more than three or four seconds. He said he saw his whole life flash before his eyes.

After the services we had a long, quiet ride back to Aabenraa. On subsequent visits to Brother Ravn, I learned that because of a heart condition, he had only taken sponge baths for the past several years. His doctor had told him never to go into water, because his heart would stop.

I finally realized why it had been so difficult to get him to recommit himself to baptism. To Brother Ravn, his baptism was going to be the ultimate commitment.

A Young Man's Awakening

KATHRYN SCHLENDORF

A young man was raised by faithful parents. They did the best they knew how to do. Were they perfect? No one is. But they tried. Family prayers were said daily. Family home evenings together were regularly held. This boy was taught the facts of the gospel, but he did not believe. He did not act on his knowledge, and it was dormant in him. In his late teens, in the 1970s, he left home and did not communicate with his family for three years. The police had his photograph and his name, and stats were filed with missing persons departments, but nothing came of the searching. He was simply gone. "What did we do wrong? What more could we have done?" The parents took the blame for their lost son.

The boy drifted from one group of companions to another. Finally he ended up outside a large metropolitan city in a commune of criminally involved individuals. They organized their robberies and their drug deals from a secluded ranch, and the authorities did not know they were there. Anyone who tried to leave the commune was beaten, often to death. This boy knew there was no turning back. It did not take long for him to realize that he had never intended for his life to get to this place. He had just drifted. Now he was in the rapids, and only deadly rocks lay ahead. . . . There was no escape.

One night, lying awake in terror, he asked himself again, "What have I done? What can I do?" An image arose in his mind. He saw his mother and father in his living room at home. They were having family home evening. He saw himself on the couch, bored, restless, eager for the lesson to be over. He heard the echo of his mother's words: "God is not distant. He loves you. He will answer your prayers." This young man had not prayed in faith for years. But he heard his mother's voice, and he knew that she believed. He rolled toward the wall, lying on the bottom bunk in a ranch house hidden in some unnamed hills. The night was pitch black. Hot tears bathed his cheeks. He could feel a symbolic wind howling and waves swelling around his heels. For the first time in his life he cried out in his mind, as Peter had, "Lord, save me!"

The words were awkward as he formed them: "Heavenly Father, my mother told me you are not far away. She believes that you are there and that you love me. Can you help me?" Can't we just imagine what that boy must have been thinking? Could all the things he had ever done have flashed across the stage of his mind? . . . [He could have wondered], Why would God love *me?* Why would he be near? Instead, he leaned on the faith of his mother and stepped out onto the water. "Lord, I believe; help thou mine unbelief."

Lying on that bunk in the pitch blackness, the boy did not have to wait long. Almost immediately words came into his mind: "Get out. Get up and leave." . . . "But how?" . . . He knew that all the men sleeping in the other bunks would hear him, would stop him, and would beat him for trying to escape. The voice returned and said, "Now." The boy turned over and sat up. He grabbed his boots and tiptoed to the door. All he heard was the snoring of the men. No one stirred. He stepped onto the porch, sure that the dogs would wake up and bark at him. They did not. He crossed the yard to the gate, opened it, pulled on his boots, and ran for all he was worth. He did not stop until he saw the lights of the highway and then only to stick out his thumb. A trucker pulled over and gave him a lift to a nearby gas station, where that boy used the phone. At two o'clock in the morning his parents' phone rang. "Mom and Dad, will you come and get me? I want to come home."

"Lord, I believe; help thou mine unbelief." The Lord is not distant, and he wants to reinforce our faith. We must take the first step. We must believe and ask. All things are possible to him that believeth—to him (or her) who walks not by sight, but by faith.

A Mother's Prayer

TERESA B. CLARK

I grew up in Maryland, in the suburbs of the nation's capital. Wheaton Regional Park was my backyard, and its wooded trails were my refuge from the storm of those wild and unsteady years in the late 1960s and early 1970s. I loved the trickling creek and hardwood trees. I loved to squeeze honey-suckle nectar from bulging blossoms. In the woods I wasn't awkward, I wasn't a disappointment, I could think and do what I wanted. My mother, however, didn't get much peace from the woods. She didn't find them to be the idyllic hideaway that I did. She told me over and over again to never go into the woods after dark. I told her to lighten up.

I was really just a typical teen—and my mother a typical mom—but I still "looked the part" of the times. I had a lava lamp, I wore hip-huggers, I listened to loud music, and my long hair hung over my face.

But one day a miracle happened that changed my perspective—and my actions.

Mother and I were arguing. It was obvious the

46

confrontation was heading nowhere fast. Her words were still echoing through the house as I ran for the door: "You just don't understand." *Neither do you,* I thought as I headed out into the growing darkness. I headed for my bike. I heard her calling after me. "Where do you think you're going," she called in vain. I pedaled as fast as I could down the hill of our backyard and into my woods. My mother's lifelong advice to stay out of the woods after dark momentarily entered my thoughts. I ignored it. *What did she know?*

I pedaled faster. I was deep into the woods, twilight fading fast behind me, when I rounded a bend and was blocked by a group of older boys. They seemed to be somewhere between seventeen and nineteen years old. I knew instantly I should flee, but they surrounded me. Suddenly, I was grabbed from behind, and the blade of a stiletto switchblade knife was pressed against my throat.

"Get off your bike."

"No."

I knew I couldn't show fear. I told myself to look tough—I could get out of this. Everything inside of me screamed: "Stay on your bike!" I was never sure what happened after that. Perhaps it was an unidentified sound. Or maybe the light made me look tougher than I really was. But suddenly, they all became very nervous. I heard a voice say, "Hey, I know her." The knife dropped, and they all ran like skittish deer. Salvation! I stood alone for a moment then pedaled home much faster than I had left.

All the way home I resolved not to say a word to my

mother. How could I admit she was right about my precious woods? I came into the house from the basement and sneaked upstairs. I didn't want her to know I was home. The house was filled with an intense quiet. I tried to ignore it, but my curiosity got the best of me. I tiptoed through the house until I reached my Mom's room. I peeked in the half-closed door.

She was on her knees, praying.

Understanding coursed over me. I hadn't stared anyone down. No one had recognized me and run. I was coming home unscathed for only one reason—the power of a mother's faith. I stood there speechless. She rose from her knees, tears pooling in her eyes as they were in mine. She didn't say a word. She just held open her arms as I ran inside.

My teen years were pretty typical after that. I wasn't perfect; neither was she. I still dressed like a hippie; she still hated it. Yet whenever I was gone from her, the image of her on her knees stayed with me—a reminder of God's unconditional love, his desire for our obedience in every situation, and the power of a mother's prayer.

Laboring in the Trenches

CARLFRED BRODERICK

$\mathcal{O}$ften the Lord has taught me through blessings; as I've had my hands on someone's head, He's taught me things I did not know and sometimes didn't want to know. The first one was a case of a sister whom I'd known for years and who, in my judgment, had made some very poor life choices. She had married a handsome, charming young man who initially wasn't a member of the Church but joined the Church for her. She waited a year to marry him and then went to the temple. It was the last time he ever went to the temple. I knew he was a flake from the beginning. Out of my wisdom, it didn't surprise me that he soon returned to many of his pre-Church habits—most of the transgressions in the book that you can think of and some that I might not have.

There was great pain for this woman. A good, good woman, she kept in the Church; she kept in the kingdom; she suffered enormous pain because her husband went back to gambling and drinking and other things that were unhappy and unwholesome. But, the greater pain came when her children, having these two models before them, began to follow him. He would say things like, "Well, you can go to church with your mother and sit through three hours of you know what, or you can come to the racetrack with me, and we'll have good stuff to eat and drink and have a great time." It was a tough choice, and very often the children chose to go with him. They gradually seemed to adopt his lifestyle, values, and attitude toward the Church and toward sacred things. Although she never wavered from her own faith and faithfulness and her commitment to her Heavenly Father, her family was slipping away from her.

As she asked me for a blessing to sustain her in what to do with this awful situation in which she found herself, my thoughts were, "Didn't you ask for this? You married a guy who really didn't have any depth to him and raised your kids too permissively. You should have fought harder to keep them in church rather than letting them run off to racetracks." I had all those judgments in my head. I laid my hands on her head, and the Lord told her of His love and His tender concern for her. He acknowledged that He had given her (and that she had volunteered for) a far, far harder task than He would like. (And, as He put in my mind, a harder task than I had had. I have eight good kids, the last of whom just went to the temple. All would have been good if they had been orphans.) She, however, had signed up for hard children, for children who had rebellious spirits but who were valuable; for a hard husband who had a rebellious spirit but who was valuable. The Lord alluded to events in her life that I hadn't known about, but which she confirmed afterwards: twice Heavenly Father had given her the choice between life and death, whether to come home and be relieved of her responsibilities, which weren't going very well, or whether to stay to see if she could work them through. Twice on death's bed she had sent the messenger away and gone back to that hard task. She stayed with it.

I repented. I realized I was in the presence of one of the Lord's great noble spirits, who had chosen not a safe place behind the lines pushing out the ordinance to the people in the front lines as I was doing, but somebody who chose to live out in the trenches where the Lord's work was being done, where there was risk, where you could be hurt, where you could lose, where you could be destroyed by your love. That's the way she had chosen to labor. . . .

Now she is doing well; one of her sons finally went on a mission. He had a bishop who took hold of him and shook him and got him to go. He went to one of those missions where people line up to be baptized when you get off the plane. He had a wonderful mission; they all but made an icon of him. He had miracles under his hands. He came back hotter than a firecracker for missions. He wouldn't leave alone his younger brother, who was planning on playing football in college instead of going on a mission, until he also went on a mission. The younger boy looked up to his brother; nobody could have turned that second kid around except his older brother. The younger went on a harder mission. He happened to have a language skill that he developed, and he turned out to be the best one at the language. He caught fire; he had spiritual experiences, and he came back red hot.

Those two boys started working with their sisters, who are harder cases; they haven't come all the way around yet. One of them looks better. One of them married a non-member, and her husband did a terrible thing—he met the missionaries and joined the Church and started putting pressure on his wife to become active. . . . I don't know—even dad may repent, who knows? You know, she may yet win them all.

The Miracle of
the Missing Notes

KIM NOVAS

*W*hen I was first invited to apply to be part of the Especially for Youth faculty, I thought it was a mistake. My husband reminded me of a line in my patriarchal blessing in which I was told that it would be my great privilege to be a teacher to the youth of the Church. "Perhaps," I reasoned to myself, "this is one of those hidden pockets I haven't discovered yet."

I had faith that if this was something my Heavenly Father wanted me to do, I could do it even though at that point in my life I didn't see how. I felt much safer singing and acting because I was sharing the words, thoughts, and feelings of others. How would I ever be able to share my *own* feelings and thoughts in a way that might teach and motivate others? Still, I had faith that God could strengthen me, so I began to fill out the application that had been sent to me.

As I went through that process I lost any courage I had mustered to that point. The application called for titles for not just one presentation, but *four*. I needed to provide main points, supporting points, and complete outlines with scripture references for *four* presentations. I had a hard time bearing my testimony in Church, let alone speaking for four hours. I'm embarrassed now to admit that the EFY faculty application forms sat on my desk for more than two years before I finally found the courage to try. After I finally completed them and sent them in, to my amazement, I was accepted!

My first assignment was at an EFY held in Indiana. As that first EFY approached, I prepared harder than I have for anything in my life. I wrote and rewrote my presentations so many times that my brain hurt. I practiced in front of the mirror, the dog, the empty living room, and even the dirty dishes in my kitchen sink. There I was quoting scriptures to dirty dishes! I read every book on speaking I could get my hands on. I wrote out the main points and references for each of my presentations on little note cards. I was scared, but I was ready.

I went to Indiana and met the EFY teachers and counselors and the youth. I became more and more nervous as the hour of my first class approached. Another teacher, Randy Bird, realized how I was feeling and was kind enough to walk me to my assigned room. He offered some much-needed and much-appreciated encouragement and support. Soon the room began to fill with young people. I smiled, shook hands, and greeted some who sat in the front. Then I went to my purse to pull out my notes—my blood, sweat, and tears. The note cards weren't there. I shook the purse and looked again. I couldn't find them anywhere. Even the printed lyrics of the new song I had planned to sing weren't there. I couldn't possibly remember all those words! I panicked as I realized I must have left them in my room. But now it was time to start, so there was nothing for me to do but swallow hard and pray. I pleaded with God to bless me as he had blessed Enoch. I reminded Heavenly Father that I was there on his errand and that I had done all I could do to prepare. Now, I needed his help to remember the main points of my presentation, the scripture references, and the song lyrics.

That very first EFY experience in Indiana was actually a little miracle for me. I felt as if God whispered to me the same message he had given Enoch: "Open thy mouth, and it shall be filled, and I will give thee utterance" (Moses 6:32). That's exactly what happened. My talks had never gone so well in all the times I'd practiced them. I actually felt as if I did better and had better eye contact with the young people because I wasn't able to bury my head in my notes. When I sang my song, the words came to my mind as if someone were whispering them to me phrase by phrase.

The Lord had answered my desperate prayer. I had no choice but to rely totally on him, and he carried me through that experience. I opened my mouth and it was filled. Forgetting my notes was the best thing that ever happened to me. With this new confidence I vowed that, although I would prepare, I would try to deliver my presentations without notes, so I could look at the young people I was teaching.

Although I consider what happened in Indiana to be a miracle, I'm sure I wasn't nearly as polished as the speakers those youth were accustomed to hearing. I'm sure that most of the young people in that room for my first EFY presentation must have wondered who had ever invited me to come. I'm sure many other young people through the years have wondered the same thing. I don't really blame them. After all, I wonder the same thing myself every time I look at the list of who is teaching with me. But I'm trying. I'm hanging in there, persevering, not giving up.

I discovered a hidden talent, had faith that Heavenly Father would help me, found the courage to try, and am now working hard to improve.

"I Will Go! I Will Do It!"

HEIDI S. SWINTON

*E*stablishing an official Church presence in Czechoslovakia had been impossible. The government officials responsible for such decisions were cold, not interested, and not attentive. For many years the request for official recognition was studied. And later, "still being studied." Then in February 1990, the key unyielding official was removed, and his successor "had ears to hear."

Elder Russell M. Nelson had for many years tried to open a dialogue with government officials in Czechoslovakia. He told of finally arriving at a time when a receptive official "heard our complete story. He said, 'Your request for recognition will be approved this very month. Your people may again worship in full dignity. Your missionaries may again return to this country.'" Official recognition was granted 21 February and became effective 1 March 1990.

The courageous efforts of the district president in Czechoslovakia, Ĵiri Ŝänederfleî, whom Elder Nelson called "the real hero of the story," were vital in the Church's obtaining official recognition. He explained:

"Some two and one-half years earlier, Elder Ringger and I had learned that recognition could be formally requested only by a Czechoslovakian member of the Church. So we went to the home of Brother and Sister Sänederfleř. We explained that we had just received that information from the chairman of the Council of Religious Affairs. Knowing that other Czechoslovakian leaders and thinkers had been imprisoned or put to death for religious or dissident belief, we told Brother Sänederfleř that we, as his Church leaders, could not and would not make that request of him. After contemplating only a brief moment, Brother Sänederfleř humbly said, 'I will go! I will do it!' As he spoke, his wife, Olga, shed a tear. They embraced and said, 'We will do whatever is needed. This is for our Lord, and His work is more important than our freedom or life.'

"Some months later, when the papers were properly prepared, Brother Sänederfleř submitted them personally. He and other members were subjected to strict surveillance. The Saints continued in courage and faith. Ultimately, after periodic fasting and prayer and complete compliance with all requirements, they received that glorious announcement of recognition. How I admire the Sänederfleřs and all those stalwart members who endured so much interrogation and risk."

Brother and Sister Sänederfleř did not rest. Brother Sänederfleř was called to preside over the Freiberg Germany Temple, beginning 1 September 1991, and Sister Sänederfleř was called as the temple matron.

A Letter Home

HUGH B. BROWN

$\mathcal{T}$he influence of the home and the faith that comes from the home was well illustrated in a letter written by an army nurse in the last World War from Africa to her parents. She said:

"It is Sunday morning, and I know you are in church. That fact, almost as sure as sunrise and springtime, is one of the chief sources of whatever courage I may have. It is not just that I know you are sitting in a certain building at a certain hour of the week, but that from my earliest childhood everything you did and encouraged me to do harmonized with, and somehow stood behind, your going to church.

"Your church attendance was not just a gesture lightly made, nor duty grimly performed. It was vital and real, the open avowal of your most cherished convictions, backed up by your daily conduct—family worship, grace at meals, individual prayers which you taught us children to say, the unfailing sympathy and courtesy which you showed to us and to each other—all summed up when we sat together there as a unit in church on Sunday morning.

"I can see the picture now—you two and us children, the light coming in through the windows, the music, the quiet peace, that is what I mean when I say it is the source of whatever courage I find at my command now under these conditions. That courage you built up within me because I learned from you and your daily experience that God is good; that right prevails even in present circumstances, even though present circumstances indicate the opposite. And oh, how I need that courage."

I shall not read the rest of her letter, but in closing she said: "I have found that thousands of the men with whom I have come in contact are sustained and helped and fortified by the faith they were taught in their homes."

Invictus

WILLIAM ERNEST HENLEY

Out of the night that covers me,
Black as the pit from pole to pole,
I thank whatever gods may be
For my unconquerable soul.

In the fell clutch of circumstance
I have not winced nor cried aloud.
Under the bludgeonings of chance
My head is bloody, but unbowed.

Beyond this place of wrath and tears
Looms but the horror of the shade,
And yet the menace of the years
Finds and shall find me unafraid.

It matters not how strait the gate,
How charged with punishments the scroll,
I am the master of my fate:
I am the captain of my soul.

The Soul's Captain:
An Answer to "Invictus"

ORSON F. WHITNEY

Art thou in truth?
Then what of him who bought thee
  with his blood?
Who plunged into devouring seas
And snatched thee from the flood?

Who bore for all our fallen race
What none but him could bear—
The God who died that man might live
And endless glory share?

Of what avail thy vaunted strength
Apart from his vast might?
Pray that his light may pierce the gloom
That thou mayest see aright.

Men are as bubbles on the wave,
As leaves upon the tree,
Thou, captain of thy soul! Forsooth,
Who gave that place to thee?

Free will is thine—free agency,
To wield for right or wrong;
But thou must answer unto him
To whom all souls belong.

Bend to the dust that "head unbowed,"
Small part of life's great whole,
And see in him and him alone,
The captain of thy soul.

Beating the Enemy

HEIDI S. SWINTON

*W*ar teaches many lessons: some on the battlefront, some in the heart. Twenty-year-old Private A. C. Christensen saw six months of combat in World War II before being captured and sent to a Japanese prison camp. Early in his captivity he was forced to relinquish almost all of his few possessions. When a guard eyed his watch, about the only thing he had left, he understood the signal. He removed the watch from his wrist and handed it over.

He spent the next three years in a daily routine of endless beatings, exhaustion, disease, and death. Hunger was his constant companion; he struggled to remember even the most simple meals of hot dogs and sauerkraut on board ship.

Like those pioneers who pushed and pulled when their feet were bare and their strength gone, their companions lost to death and disease, somehow he carried on.

But eventually that strength began to wane, and finally he found himself slipping toward death as so many of his fellow soldiers had done. "They weren't necessarily the sickest among us," he recalled, "but they would lie in their beds in a semifetal position and stare at nothing." At morning bed check they were dead.

"Death began to seem more and more like my only release. One day I put down my hammer and told the guard I would not work any longer. I didn't care what he did to me. I wanted to die. He beat me, and afterwards, as I lay in my bed waiting for the end to come, I took out the two precious pieces of paper I had managed to keep concealed for three years: one was a picture of my parents, the other was my patriarchal blessing.

"As I read my blessing, I thought of my grandfather, the patriarch who had given me the blessing, and my dear mother, who had patiently taken down every word. The words softened me. Maybe there was a future for me after all. Then I studied my parents' faces in the picture. I began to recall my childhood, our farm, my brother Max, and the times we had spent riding our horses.

"I started to pray. Somehow I began to feel strengthened. I remembered that Helaman's army of two thousand had been strengthened by their mothers' teachings. I remembered my mother's words to me and my brother, both still in our late teens. She promised us that if we would always live the Word of Wisdom, the Lord would bless us.

"As I lay there thinking about what my mother had said, I weighed only eighty-five pounds. I didn't feel that I could run and not be weary, but maybe I could walk

and not faint. That day my spirits lifted, and I determined that I would hang on.

"I had beaten my enemy."

Do What Is Right

Any Objections?

ROBERT L. SIMPSON

My heart was touched . . . as I had the privilege of reading an excerpt from a serviceman's letter to his parents. As I read, I realized that his training instructor had made it a habit of starting each day's discussion with a few off-color stories.

One morning, quite by surprise, the instructor asked if anyone objected to a couple of "*good*" stories before starting the day's instruction. This young Mormon boy said that almost as though he had been ejected from his seat by an unseen power, he shot up and said, "Yes, sir, *I* object."

After a long stony silence, the instructor said, "Are there any others?" You can imagine the feelings of this boy's heart as one by one another dozen or so young army recruits stood in defense of what they really believed. Those standing were invited to leave the class, and then halfway out, they were called back with a comment from the instructor, "I guess we can skip the stories this morning."

Wouldn't you like the privilege of shaking hands with

that kind of Aaronic Priesthood courage? Isn't it gratifying to know that you don't have to turn the pages of history back twenty-six hundred years to find the courage of a Nephi or a Daniel in the lions' den or a David meeting Goliath? And isn't it also gratifying to know that for every courageous heart with a fortitude to stand up and be counted, there will be a host of others willing to rally to the cause of truth and right?

Mrs. America

VIVIAN R. CLINE

$\mathcal{T}$he year 1980] was a difficult year for many Church members. It was the year that the Equal Rights Amendment had been proposed to Congress. . . . Though the Church never takes a stand on political issues, it does take stands on moral issues, and in this case the Brethren saw moral implications and recommended that we not support the amendment in its poorly written and easily misinterpreted form. The Church received a lot of publicity because of that stand—and not necessarily positive publicity. . . .

[That year, I won the Mrs. Utah Pageant.] The nationals, however, were a different ball game from the Utah experience. I was now competing against forty-nine other winners who all had the same sparkle in their eyes.

Ten grueling days of competition followed. . . . The final area of competition was the personal interview. This is where you either made it or lost it, because it counted for 50 percent of the total points.

I clearly remember that day and how nervous I was. I

couldn't even sit down. Pacing back and forth, I would watch the contestants who preceded me come out of the personal interview room. One of them came out with tears in her eyes, and I knew then that this part of the competition was going to be really tough.

Suddenly I heard the words that made my whole body shiver. "Mrs. Utah, please come in." . . .

To my surprise I felt more calm and comfortable than I had supposed I could be. My thoughts were clear, my words crisp. I answered questions regarding my career and the sole question they asked about my family. I felt totally at ease. . . .

All at once the national director said, "Time is up." Four minutes had gone fast. As I started to get up from my chair, I felt good and knew that I had done well.

Then it happened. A hand came straight up in front of me as one of the women judges said: "Excuse me for asking this question, Mrs. Utah, but you are from Utah. Are you a Mormon?" . . .

I didn't pause or hesitate when the question was asked, but proudly responded, "Yes, I am."

The judge now asked, "Tell me, why is your church prejudiced against blacks?"

I was dumbfounded. I couldn't believe she had asked such a question. Quickly I told her that we were not prejudiced against blacks, that many members of the Church were black, and we had missions in Africa. . . .

It was beginning to get very warm in that room. Another judge now joined the attack with: "Do you really believe everything the Mormon church teaches? I mean, everything?"

Calmly I answered: "Yes, I do. One hundred percent."

Then the big question came. A famous motion picture producer demanded, "Why did you recently excommunicate a woman from your church just because she believes in ERA?"

This one I was really ready for. I had read all the Church publications on the Equal Rights Amendment and had stayed abreast of media reports on what was going on. I was well aware of the instance he referred to.

"The woman you mention was excommunicated not for her belief in ERA but for other reasons," I explained. "If a person is a member of your club and he doesn't support the president of your club nor the by-laws, you don't let him remain a member, now, do you?"

In a very heated and agitated manner the producer said, "I believe I'm the one asking the questions."

"No," I said, "you would not."

By this time the national director was about to have a cardiac arrest. . . . Hurriedly she said: "It's time to go. We must go now."

Again I began to rise from my chair. I stood tall, smiled, and made for the door. Then I heard one last question.

"Tell me, Mrs. Utah," the fiery producer asked, "do *you* believe in ERA?"

I couldn't believe my ears. The audacity this man had, questioning my integrity! He knew that only the panel of judges, the national director, and I were in that room. He knew that, like the other contestants, I wanted that national crown. It would have been so easy to tell him what he wanted to hear.

With my back straight and my head held high I looked into his face and said with a smile, "No."

He rolled his eyes up to the ceiling in disgust as I left the room.

Outside in the waiting area the other contestants ran up to me and asked me how it had gone. I smiled and calmly said: "It was great. You're going to love it. It was a breeze." Then I went back to my hotel room, called my mother long-distance . . . and cried my heart out. . . .

The next morning the national director approached me at rehearsal and . . . told me: "The judges came to me after the personal interview session yesterday and said that they had come down on you pretty hard. If you would like a formal apology from them they will be happy to give you one."

Quickly I told the director that my concern was that they judge me according to the way I had responded to the questions and not on my personal and religious views. She assured me that they would.

Wanting to believe her, I quietly added, "How do you think I did?"

Looking around to make sure no one was listening, she whispered, "Personally, darling, I think you did a _____ good job."

That was all I needed to know. Again I felt confident that all was well. The final event came the next evening. There the names of the ten finalists would be called out and the selection of the queen and the runners-up would be made. . . .

The announcer began calling out the names of the finalists. When he got to the third name, suddenly something whispered to me, "Vivian, keep your back straight and your head high, because your name will not be called." . . .

Contestants number four, five, and six were called. I began to get a little nervous. Number seven and eight. I swallowed hard. Number nine. I took a deep breath. And contestant number ten . . . My name was not read. I believe that one of the most difficult things I have ever had to do in my life was to stand in front of national television with a smile on my face when my heart was at my feet. . . .

Luckily for me, my dear sweet husband was there at the pageant to console and comfort me. I don't know what I would have done without him. . . .

I may have left a pageant in Las Vegas, Nevada, without a crown, but that experience and the rewards that resulted will far outlast a few cheap rhinestones. For you see, I am resolved that I *will* have the moral courage to make my actions consistent with my knowledge of right and wrong.

Living the Truth

JACK R. CHRISTIANSON

$\mathscr{F}$or the evening session of [youth] conference I was assigned to speak on the sensitive topic of music and how it affects us, a subject I had addressed many times previously.

As I was approaching the speaking arena earlier in the day, my stereo and briefcase in hand, I noticed four young men listening to some music. They saw me and immediately recognized me as someone different. I was dressed in a suit and tie and was carrying a stereo tape deck.

As I drew closer to them, the one holding the stereo set it down and started walking towards me. Though small in stature, he was very noticeable and appeared somewhat out of place at an LDS youth conference. His hair was unique. It was a conglomerate of styles. Hanging from his left ear was a cross earring. He wore a black leather jacket with a small chain hanging over one shoulder. Both wrists were covered with spiked wrist bands. His T-shirt had obviously been purchased at a concert he had attended—it bore the logo of the band that had performed.

As he came closer, I said hello. . . . Without any hesitation he poked me in the chest and blurted, "Are you the chump that's going to tell us all our rock 'n' roll music is bad and if we listen to heavy metal we're all going to hell?"

I was shocked. In disbelief I told him that I was the speaker and that I would share with him how to choose what music to listen to and how music affects our actions, feelings, thoughts, and spirituality, but that he would have to make his own decisions. Without waiting for more, he poked me in the chest a second time and asked basically the same question: Would he go to hell if he listened to heavy-metal music.

I responded by asking him to please refrain from poking me again. As the words were falling from my lips, his finger was already on the way to my chest. "Listen," he said as the finger made contact a third time, "if you tell me my heavy-metal music or my rock 'n' roll is bad, I will get up and leave your discussion." In my mind, I reasoned if that was all it took, he was as good as gone. He walked away, somewhat jokingly saying, "I'll leave! I'll leave!"

Later on that evening, the time came to speak on music. When I reached the pulpit and looked at the audience, there he was, sitting on the second row, arms folded and eyes glaring the message, "Go ahead, try to teach me or make me change." I spoke for some time before I reached the point of teaching how to choose between what is "good" and what is "bad." I quoted some verses from the seventh chapter of Moroni. While doing so, some words from the film *Man's Search for Happiness* came racing into my mind: "Only if you are unafraid of truth will you ever find it." As I said the phrase, the words rang through the hall and into many hearts. I stopped, pointed at the young man, and repeated the phrase, insinuating that he was afraid of the truth and that it would elude him forever if he continued to fear it. I then asked the congregation . . . "Do you have the courage it takes to live truth?" . . .

As I left the building . . . , I saw the young man standing behind a tree. My heart began pounding with anticipation as he approached me. His voice was soft and subdued. He asked if we could spend a few minutes talking before I retired. That few minutes turned into nearly three hours. After finding a place to sit and talk, I learned his name. He said he didn't want to wait . . . to talk because he might lose his courage. . . . We talked. We cried. I learned.

He told me that for the first time in his life, he asked himself if he was afraid of the truth. He found that he was terrified. I asked why, and his threefold answer revealed a frightened but courageous young man. He said if he lived the truth, he would have to give up most of his friends because they were all involved in drugs and alcohol. I asked if he had been. He hung his head and wept as he told of his involvement.

Then he said if he lived the truth, he would have to get rid of all his music because it made him feel exactly the way he wanted to feel—angry. He explained his situation with his parents and how deeply he wanted to get back at one of them.

He went on to explain that if he lived the truth, he might have to go see his bishop. He explained some of his problems, and I assured him that he needed to go as soon as possible. He wanted to have the courage necessary to face and live truth, but he also realized the difficulty of change. He realized the necessity to sacrifice temporary pleasures for true eternal principles and peace.

As we sat talking and weeping together, both of us realized how difficult it is to live truth when so many are mocking and fearing it. We made some special promises to each other and then embraced. As I held this aching young man in my arms and listened to his sobs and pleadings for help to live truth, I determined that any price was worth paying in order to help him. He couldn't do it alone—he knew it and I felt it.

Much time has passed since that night in the forest. But I have never forgotten the pleading eyes and the quavering voice that asked so trustingly for help to live truth. To help ourselves and our loved ones return to our Father, we must never fear truth.

God Make Me a Man

HARLAN GOLDSBURY METCALF

Give me the strength to stand for right
When other folks have left the fight.
Give me the courage of the man
Who knows that if he will, he can.
Teach me to see in every face
The good, the kind and not the base.
Make me sincere in word and deed
Blot out from me all shame and greed
Help me to guard my troubled soul
By constant, active self-control.
Clean up my thoughts, my work, my play
And keep me pure from day to day.
O make of me a man.

Standing As
a Daughter of God

LEANN P. WHEELER

*W*hile I was attending law school in New Jersey, the National Organization of Women was picketing our ward and demonstrating against the Church. My bishop asked me to assist as a spokeswoman for LDS women in our area. One night he called to tell me that the former wife of a regional representative was speaking at a well-publicized NOW meeting in my neighborhood. She intended to speak against the Church and its priesthood leaders. Would I please attend?

When I arrived at the meeting, the room was packed with at least a hundred women. I noticed four or five other LDS women from our area, some of whom knew the speaker personally. As the meeting progressed, the speaker vented her frustration with the Church, offering her opinion that a Mormon's idea of heaven is to keep women barefoot and pregnant for eternity and that Mormon women have no freedom over their own lives. The crowd grew indignant. Suddenly she paused, looked around, and said, "In fact, there are Mormon women in this audience right now, sent by their bishops to spy on this meeting."

I have never felt such a swell of animosity. It was an actual physical force, like electricity crackling, then an uproar, with women yelling, "Who are they? We want to know who they are. Stand up, stand up!"

A voice within said, "Stand up!" I sat very still and thought, "You have got to be kidding." The voice, which was neither still nor small to my hearing, came again. "Stand up." I took a deep breath and stood up.

Dead silence.

"Well," I said, since I had their attention, "I live here in Maplewood. A few of you are my neighbors." I had seen one neighbor and assumed there were others present. "I am a Mormon, and I am pregnant," I said, because I was eight months pregnant, "but I am not barefoot. I am a third-year law student and an editor of our *Law Review,* and I have the full support and encouragement not only of my husband but of my bishop." I was very calm.

"Sit down," several women yelled. I sat down, gladly. Then others called out, "Let her talk."

I cannot recall anything specific said after that, but the process of being asked to sit and then being invited to speak again was repeated at least twice. The second time I spoke seven or eight minutes about the role of women in the Church. The speaker, out of time, said little else beyond inviting anyone with questions to come up afterwards. In effect, her accusation had ended her remarks.

After the meeting, several women, distinctly within

my hearing but under their breath, called me a liar, but several others stopped to thank me for my comments. One woman apologized and said how uncomfortable she felt about what had been said, especially in attacking another church.

It was a humbling experience for me. By standing when the Spirit commanded, however, I know I was directed in what to say to that gathering of concerned women. Even if my comments accomplished little else, at least those present had a chance to hear a different perspective.

"Get Behind Me, Satan!"

JOHN A. WIDTSOE

*S*he [Anna Widtsoe] had not been taught the Word of Wisdom, except as it had been mentioned casually in her gospel conversations. Now, she began to understand its real meaning and purpose and the necessity of obeying it, as it was the desire of the Father that his children should heed it. Like nearly all of her country people she had drunk coffee from her childhood and was an occasional user of tea. Alcoholic beverages she did not use. She set about to give up the use of tea and coffee but found it difficult. When she sewed every night far beyond midnight, the cup of coffee seemed to freshen her, she thought. After a two months' struggle she came home one day, having given serious consideration to the Word of Wisdom problem. Her mind was made up. She stood in the middle of the room and said aloud, "Never again. Get behind me, Satan!" and walked briskly to her cupboard, took out the packages of coffee and tea, and threw them on the fire. From that day she never used tea or coffee.

A Glass of Lemonade

DAVID O. MCKAY

When I visited the beautiful island of Tahiti in 1921 I learned of an incident associated with Brother Vaio (a member of the Church), who was then captain of one of the government schooners.

The newly appointed governor of the island was to make a tour of inspection of a government-owned vessel. Captain Vaio and his associates decorated their ship, placed fruits and delicacies on the table, and made ready for a suitable and appropriate reception to his excellency. A glass of wine was placed at each plate with which at the proper time all would respond to the toast and drink to the health of the governor. There was one exception however—at Captain Vaio's plate there was placed a glass of lemonade. One of his associates protested saying that he would offend the governor if he drank only lemonade at the toast, but notwithstanding these protestations Brother Vaio insisted that he would drink only lemonade when the toast was proposed.

It was Captain Vaio's responsibility and honor to

make the welcome speech. This he did, and at the conclusion he explained in substance:

"Your Excellency, before proposing the toast I wish to explain why I am drinking lemonade instead of the customary wine. I am a member of The Church of Jesus Christ of Latter-day Saints. Every Sunday morning I teach a class of young people. It is one of our tenets not to drink wine or strong drink, tea, nor coffee, nor use tobacco. I cannot consistently tell them not to use intoxicating liquor and then indulge myself; therefore, you will understand why on this occasion I am drinking lemonade. And now I propose a toast to the health and happiness of his Excellency, governor of Tahiti."

There was a tense silence among the ship's crew as the Governor arose to make his response. He was a true gentleman and appreciated the loyalty and manhood of the man who had given the welcoming speech. In substance the governor said:

"Captain Vaio, I thank you and your associates for this hearty welcome, and I am glad to learn that you maintain the ideals of your Church in regard to temperance. I wish we had more men with such sterling character to take charge of the government's ships."

As we sailed that evening toward Rarotonga, I wondered in admiration how many of the members of the Church were as loyal to the ideals and teachings of the gospel as was Captain Vaio. . . .

I have learned that Captain Vaio has gone to his eternal reward. Perhaps he knows how many times I have told this story to Sunday School children, not a few of whom let us hope have been encouraged along the pathway of duty, because of his courage and loyalty to what he knew was right.

A Life without Drugs

BILL STEWART

$\mathcal{I}$ started going to church again. Mostly it was because Jeff and Linda, and of course Tammy, were there every Sunday. But it wasn't just a Sunday thing for them. They talked a lot about the Church even on dates, which I could hardly believe. They were very casual about it, but it came into the conversation quite a bit. . . .

I started . . . praying that I would get the help I needed to get by without drugs. I think it really helped. Tammy and I started dating pretty regularly, and after a while I started to feel like she was the one for me. I knew she was a strict Mormon, but that didn't worry me because I was pretty much off the drugs and I was going to church and praying. I was actually more religious than I'd ever been before. Finally I started hinting around about how the two of us might get married. One day, Tammy came out and said to me, "Look, Bill, you're twenty-one years old." I said, "Yeah, so what?" And she said, "If you're going to go on a mission, you'd better do it soon. The older you get, the harder it is to make the decision." I almost dropped dead. Tammy knew about my drug problem, and she knew I'd never even thought about a mission since I was nineteen. But every time I would try to talk to her about our future together, she would say, "Well, let's wait to see whether or not you decide to go on a mission."

One day I decided that since I really believed the Church was true and because it was helping me get over my drug problem, I owed it to God to go. I realized that one of the reasons I didn't want to serve a mission was that I knew once I went I wouldn't be able to get drugs or alcohol easily. Even though I was trying my best not to take anything—and doing better at it all the time— the thought of not being *able* to get drugs if I "needed" them was pretty scary. Also, I knew I would have to confess to the bishop, and I didn't want to do that. I still felt like no one had the right to judge me. I was pretty proud. But one morning, when I realized that I *should* go on a mission, I finally said this little prayer, sort of like, "Oh, all right, get off my back. I'll go, I'll go!" It was a really moving prayer, you can tell.

The funny thing was, from that time on there was a real difference in my life. All of a sudden I seemed to need a lot less Dutch courage to get through things. I felt like I was kind of being carried along. It was strange. I went to the bishop, and he put me on probation and asked me how long it would take me to earn the money for my mission. I said about six months. The bishop said, "Well, then, let's work together during that time and get you all ready to go!" It felt good. He was really nice, not at all like I expected.

I worked for six months and kept going to my hospital

group and dating Tammy and calling home and checking in with the bishop, and the drug problem just sort of lost its hold on me somehow. . . .

The six months went by, and I got my mission call to the Southern California Spanish-speaking mission. If you'd told me two years ago that I could learn another language, I wouldn't have believed you. If you'd put me in a class and told me I had to learn Spanish in two months, I would have stoked myself up on so many drugs you would have had to prop me up with two-by-fours just to keep me from slithering off my chair. But my mission has been a great experience. I've learned even more about the power of prayer and service to others and what they can do in your life. I feel like my family and Tammy are proud of me, and I want to make them even prouder. I don't know whether or not I was right about not being able to get drugs on my mission, because I've never tried. I'm just too busy to think about it! Now I can see that the drugs were a substitute for the Spirit and for service to other people. And those things are free. You can't beat that.

But a
Small Moment

Adversity

WILLIAM SHAKESPEARE

$\mathscr{S}$weet are the uses of adversity,

Which, like the toad, ugly and venomous,

Wears yet a precious jewel in his head.

Into the Lion's Den

WILLIAM E. BERRETT

$\mathscr{T}$he story of two young men, Denison L. Harris and Robert Scott, shows something of the nature of the conspiracy within the Church against the Prophet [Joseph Smith]:

These two young men, then but seventeen years of age, had been invited to attend a secret meeting of the conspirators. In a spirit of comradeship they confided in each other, wondering what course to pursue. They took the matter to Denison's father, Emer Harris, brother of Martin Harris. He advised them to lay the whole matter before Joseph Smith. The Prophet requested the two boys to attend the meeting and report to him its proceedings.

The meeting was held on the Sabbath day at the house of William Law, counselor to the Prophet. A multitude of charges were laid against Joseph and Hyrum Smith. . . .

The two boys were silent observers and, after the meeting was over, met the Prophet secretly and reported to him. Following the Prophet's advice they attended similar meetings the two following Sundays, and received an invitation to attend a fourth meeting. In each meeting the spirit of bitterness against the Prophet increased. Before they attended the last meeting Joseph Smith said to them:

"This will be your last meeting; this will be the last time that they will admit you into their councils! They will come to some determination. But be sure that you make no covenants nor enter into any obligations, whatever, with them." After a pause he added, "Boys, this will be their last meeting, and they may shed your blood, but I hardly think they will, as you are so young. If they do I will be a lion in their path! Don't flinch. If you have to die; die like men. You will be martyrs to the cause and your crowns can be no greater. But I hardly think they will shed your blood."

When Denison and Robert approached the house of William Law on that Sabbath afternoon they were stopped at the door by armed guards. After a severe questioning and cross-examination they were admitted.

The house was filled with men, pouring out charges against the Prophet. Bitterness was everywhere. It was evident that a decision would be arrived at during the meeting. As the two boys took no part in the discussions but remained by themselves, William Law and Austin Cowles spent some time explaining to them how the Prophet had fallen and why they should join in ridding the Church of him. As the meeting progressed, each member present was requested to take oath as follows:

"You solemnly swear, before God, and all the Holy Angels, and these your brethren by whom you are surrounded, that you will give your life, your liberty, your influence, your all, for the destruction of Joseph Smith and his party, so help you God."

The person being sworn would then say "I do," after which he signed his name in the presence of the justice of the peace.

About two hundred took oath. Among them were three women heavily veiled, who testified to attempts by Joseph and Hyrum to seduce them. When all but the two boys had complied, the attention of the group was turned to them. The boys refused to take the oath and started to leave the room. One of the number stepped in their way, exclaiming:

"No, not by a d—n sight. You know all our plans and arrangements, and we don't propose that you should leave in that style. You've got to take the oath or you'll never leave here alive."

The boys were in a dangerous position. Threatening could be heard on every hand. One voice shouted, "Dead men tell no tales." Violent hands were laid on them. Swords and bowie knives were drawn. One of the leading men said, "If you do not take that oath, we will cut your throats."

Only the wisdom of the leader prevented their murder then and there. The house of William Law stood close to the street and there was danger that the disturbance would be heard by passers-by. Better to execute them in the cellar.

Accordingly, a guard with a drawn sword and bowie knife was placed on either side of the boys, while two others armed with cocked muskets and bayonets at their backs, brought up the rear, as they were marched off in the direction of the cellar. William and Wilson Law, Austin Cowles, and others accompanied them to that place. Before committing the murderous deed, however, they gave the boys one last chance for their lives. One of them said, "Boys, if you will take that oath your lives will be spared; but you know too much for us to allow you to go free and, if you are determined to refuse, we will have to shed your blood." With their death as the immediate alternative the two boys grimly refused to turn against their Prophet. Trembling and white with fear they awaited the sword. As the sword was raised by an angry participant, a sharp voice from the crowd halted it in midair.

"Hold on! Hold on there! Let's talk this matter over before their blood is shed." A hurried consultation followed, during which the young men were relieved to hear a strong voice say, "The boy's parents very likely know where they are, and if they do not return home, strong suspicion will be aroused, and they may institute a search that would be very dangerous to us." That counsel prevailed. The boys were threatened with death if they revealed a word of what had transpired, and sent away. A guard accompanied them for a distance to prevent some of the more bloodthirsty individuals following to kill them. The parting words of the guards were, "Boys, if you ever open your mouths concerning anything you have seen or heard in any of our meetings, we will kill you by night or by day, wherever we find you, and consider it our duty."

The boys continued to the river bank, where they met the Prophet, who had become anxious and had gone in search of them. Retiring to a secluded spot below the Prophet's home they told the entire story. The bravery and loyalty of the two young men melted the Prophet to tears. For fear that harm might come to them he urged them to promise never to reveal their story for twenty years. This secrecy was faithfully kept.

The heroism of two boys saved the life of the Prophet for a time from the net closing about him. Subsequently, the conspirators were excommunicated from the Church, after which they openly allied themselves with all those forces seeking its overthrow.

Midnight in a
Missouri Dungeon

PARLEY P. PRATT

In one of those tedious nights we had lain as if in sleep till the hour of midnight had passed, and our ears and hearts had been pained, while we had listened for hours to the obscene jests, the horrid oaths, the dreadful blasphemies and filthy language of our guards, Colonel Price at their head, as they recounted to each other their deeds of rapine, murder, robbery, etc., which they had committed among the *"Mormons"* while at Far West and vicinity. They even boasted of defiling by force wives, daughters and virgins, and of shooting or dashing out the brains of men, women and children.

I had listened till I became so disgusted, shocked, horrified, and so filled with the spirit of indignant justice that I could scarcely refrain from rising upon my feet and rebuking the guards; but had said nothing to Joseph, or any one else, although I lay next to him and knew he was awake. On a sudden he arose to his feet, and spoke in a voice of thunder, or as the roaring lion, uttering, as near as I can recollect, the following words:

"SILENCE, ye fiends of the infernal pit. In the name of Jesus Christ I rebuke you, and command you to be still; I will not live another minute and bear such language. Cease such talk, or you or I die THIS INSTANT!"

He ceased to speak. He stood erect in terrible majesty. Chained, and without a weapon; calm, unruffled and dignified as an angel, he looked upon the quailing guards, whose weapons were lowered or dropped to the ground; whose knees smote together, and who, shrinking into a corner, or crouching at his feet, begged his pardon, and remained quiet till a change of guards.

I have seen the ministers of justice, clothed in magisterial robes, and criminals arraigned before them, while life was suspended on a breath, in the Courts of England; I have witnessed a Congress in solemn session to give laws to nations; I have tried to conceive of kings, of royal courts, of thrones and crowns; and of emperors assembled to decide the fate of kingdoms, but dignity and majesty have I seen but *once,* as it stood in chains, at midnight, in a dungeon in an obscure village of Missouri.

"Life Has a Fair Number
of Challenges in It"

ELEANOR KNOWLES

$\mathcal{O}$n February 7 the Hunters went to the Brigham Young University campus, where President [Howard W.] Hunter was scheduled to speak at a nineteen-stake fireside. Nearly twenty thousand young adults poured into the Marriott Center on campus, and thousands more gathered at Church buildings throughout North America for special transmission of the fireside via satellite.

After the invocation and introductions, President Hunter went to the microphone and began to speak. Suddenly a voice yelled out, "Stop right there!" A man carrying a briefcase in one hand and a black object in the other rushed out of the audience and onto the stage. Declaring that he had a bomb and a detonator, he ordered everyone except President Hunter to leave.

Most of the officials and guests quickly left the stage, but President Hunter remained, with two personal security guards who refused to leave his side. Waving the so-called detonator, which many spectators feared was a gun, the man handed a prepared statement to President Hunter and demanded that he read it. President Hunter calmly but firmly refused to do so.

In areas where audiences had assembled to watch the fireside telecast, the screens suddenly went black and a "technical difficulties" notice replaced the image and sound. At the Marriott Center, members of the audience sat stunned momentarily. Then some broke into tears; others began moving toward the exits; and a few angrily converged toward the stage area, where they tried to get the man to surrender. A modicum of calm was restored when a few students, soon joined by the entire audience, began to sing "We Thank Thee, O God, for a Prophet" and then "I Am a Child of God."

On the stage an older man tried to distract the assailant but was pushed back into a row of chairs. Then one of the angry students near the front sprayed the intruder with a can of mace, and security officers managed to wrestle him off the stand, where other students helped to subdue him.

In the confusion, President Hunter's grandnephew, Corey Child, rushed from his seat in the fifth row to the opposite side of the stand, put his hand on his uncle's chest from behind, and, whispering reassurances, helped the security guards lower him to the floor. Corey, who cracked some ribs and pulled muscles in his shoulder and knee in the confusion, looked around to see what had happened to his date. A nurse, she had followed him to the stage, and he was surprised to see her kneeling beside President Hunter.

The entire incident took about ten minutes, but to

many it seemed much longer. Finally, after resting for a few moments, President Hunter again went to the microphone and began reading his prepared talk. "Life has a fair number of challenges in it," he read. Looking out at the audience, he added, "as demonstrated." And he continued on, speaking calmly and deliberately, as though nothing had happened.

A Life Well Lived

SPENCER W. KIMBALL

$\mathcal{I}$n the recent past, I found honor and integrity in resplendent glory. I saw the trials of life multiply and culminate in a visit from the grim reaper. She was a young schoolteacher, just reaching her majority. While decorating a Christmas tree, she had fallen from the ladder and broken her back and was consigned the rest of her life to a wheelchair. In her resourcefulness, she developed her memory through the years and became a reviewer of books, for which she received compensation to support herself. No vulgar books would she read or review. Time passed, and, from her wheelchair, she enthralled her numerous audiences. A book a month she absorbed, mastered, and made hers, and then she entertained her public. Years passed.

Illness came to her widowed sister who was bedridden. The wheelchair victim, from her captivity, waited upon the sister. And now her aging mother fell and broke her hip, and with two patients, this wheelchair nurse operated a miniature hospital. They both finally died and left her alone.

In the home, she carried on. Books and books—readings and readings. Her strong, clear voice was a call to courage. Her persistence in spite of many handicaps showed an indomitable will. No pity did she ask, nor succor, nor sympathy. She first read the book, wrote a condensation, then memorized the latter. Years passed. Her overworked vocal cords eventually became hoarse and with it the means of her living was threatened. She used her precious voice as long as she could; then came the day when the hoarseness was diagnosed as the treacherous cancer. Still smiling, in her wheelchair, she asked nothing, finally giving up her reviews, then taking to her bed, with her voice petering out and her breath shortening; then to the hospital for short days of gasping; then to her grave. There was no blame, no bitterness, no moroseness, but smiles and thanks and gratitude. Facing sure death, she yet had no complaint, only sweetness and courage. THAT IS INTEGRITY. Like Job of old, she knew that her Redeemer liveth.

I Keep Going
One Day at a Time

ANNA MARIE PERKINS

$\mathcal{O}$n 12 April 1985, I received a phone call from
Galen's high school track coach saying that my son had
collapsed of sunstroke and that an ambulance was taking him to the hospital.

I got to the emergency room and saw Galen lying on
a gurney in his track uniform and shoes. He had tears
in his eyes and a look of fear. He knew something was
terribly wrong. I asked what was wrong but no one
would tell me anything for a time. I called my husband,
Richard, but he wasn't in his office. I called our former
bishop to give Galen a blessing. Then the hospital staff
informed me they had called for the Life Flight helicop-
ter to take Galen to Primary Children's Medical Center.
When Richard and I got to the hospital, the doctor
explained to us that Galen had had a massive stroke on
the left side of his brain. We cried and fell to our knees
to plead and petition the Lord to save our dear son.

Galen was in the hospital for the next six weeks.
He could not utter a word—his right side was totally

paralyzed. We were devastated and frightened. How could such a terrible thing happen? My heart ached for Galen and how this would change his life and mine.

No one ever prepares you for the duty of handling a crisis twenty-four hours a day, day in and day out. The hours are long and stressful—your life changed forever. The only way I learned to deal with our situation was one minute, one hour, and one day at a time.

Then, on 27 August 1992, seven years after Galen's stroke, Richard and I were awakened with a telephone call from Cottonwood Hospital telling us that our daughter, Tami, had been in a car accident. She was alive. Would we come? The nightmare began again.

A horrible sight awaited us in the emergency room. Our precious Tami was lying there in blood, dirt, and weeds. She was crying and talking but motionless. We learned that the three girls who had been riding in the backseat were not wearing seat belts. The car had rolled two and one-half times. Tami was thrown halfway out of the back window.

Tami's spinal cord had been stretched, and disks three and four had been injured. She was totally paralyzed from the neck down. *Paralyzed*—what a wrenching word!

Why not me? I wondered. *Why couldn't this have happened to me instead of our two beautiful children? I'd trade places with them if only I could.* They were both so young and had just begun living their lives.

With Tami's tragedy, the outpouring of love, faith, prayers, concern, compassion, fasting, visits, flowers, meals, cards, and hugs was overwhelming. Our family and friends were our lifelines once again. We felt the faith and prayers uttered in our behalf. We were grateful for our names being placed on the prayer rolls in temples throughout the country.

Since those first days after the accident, many people have said that they don't know how we have done what we have done or how we can stand it on a day-to-day basis. Well, to us, there is no choice. We have to do what we have to do. We love our children. Many times we've held hands and prayed for peace, understanding, strength, and a miracle. I try not to dwell on the negative.

It is now 2001. There has been much tribulation—much more than is told here—but after the tribulation, blessings have come. Tami is still a quadriplegic and Galen still suffers the effects of the stroke. But both have tremendous attitudes and have made much progress. And neither one lives with us or is dependent on us as much as we had anticipated.

In 1996, Tami met Russ. Russ told us later that he saw Tami's beautiful face and felt her sparkling personality and smile before he ever noticed the wheelchair. They dated and were married. In 1999, Galen was asked on a date by a wonderful young woman, Lyndie, with whom he worked. They dated for about nine months and were married. Wow! Both children married to incredible people.

For Christmas of 1999 Tami and Russ gave us the news that they were expecting a baby. We were overcome with awe. In August, Tami gave birth to the most beautiful baby girl ever. They named her Samantha

Marie. Galen and Lyndie are expecting a baby girl this fall. Richard and I are grandparents, something we didn't think was a possibility five years ago. We believe in miracles.

So, when people say to me, "Anna Marie, how do you do it?" I respond, "I just do it. I just keep going a day at a time. There is no choice. You have to pick yourself up and go on." You do what you have to do. One day at a time. And, eventually, the miracles come.

Grateful for Pain? Never! Never?

LARENE GAUNT

*P*ain is simply a part of life yet it has the amazing power to bring back the past. It is always a surprise when a simple event triggers the painful past with its pile of faded photos and retrieves them with shocking reality. That's what happened to me one hot afternoon in July when my daughter and I buried the duck eggs.

I was excited but a little confused when eggs began appearing in our yard. "One of these ducks must be a male," I said to my daughter.

"I thought male ducks had green heads. Henrietta and Millicent are just brown."

"I know. It doesn't make sense does it?"

It wasn't long until Henrietta had built a large nest beneath the lilac bush. It was deep and soft with layers of feathers, leaves, and grass. She sat on a dozen eggs all day, every day. She stayed even while the sprinklers ran leaving beads of water on her feathered back.

Every evening she waddled carefully out of the sheltered nest and gently turned each egg with her bill.

Then she fluffed a layer of nesting over the eggs, lovingly, like a hand-stitched patchwork quilt.

Despite her gentle devotion, Henrietta was crabby while she was off the nest. All she did was quack. Once I ventured near the lilac bush to take a peek at her brood. Henrietta ran toward me with her head lowered, quacking with wings crossed and tail feathers ruffled.

"What a protective mother you are," I said to her as I stepped away from the nest and Henrietta pecked at my feet. "I'm as excited as you are to get these babies here." In our innocence, ignorant of the fact that the eggs were sterile, both of us were hopeful, protective, and expectant of new life.

Millicent seemed lonely for about three weeks until, to our surprise, she built a nest in the daisies. Then I realized we had two female ducks. I called the veterinarian.

"Well, Mrs. Gaunt. All female birds lay eggs with or without a male bird around."

"Oh," I muttered. "So these eggs won't hatch."

"That's right."

I felt a sense of loss as I wandered outside. I peered through the lilacs, its flowers past blooming, at Henrietta sitting on her treasure with determination and unconditional love. I glanced over to the daisies, just ready to bloom, and there sat Millicent—the picture of the resplendent anticipation of motherhood. I simply couldn't disturb their nesting and nurturing.

"Let's just let things run their course," I said to my daughter. But I felt a nudge of pain as I realized the hopelessness amid the naive hopefulness.

A week later our dog came inside reeking of rotten eggs. Bits of white shell mixed with golden yolk were matted in her fur. So much for letting nature run its course.

"The time has come," I said to my daughter. "The eggs have to go."

We picked up the shovel, and headed for the nests. I dug a hole under the lilac bush while my daughter shooed Henrietta away. Henrietta quacked, raised up to her full height, and beat her wings at us. I leaned on my shovel and smiled until I looked past her flapping wings and caught a glimpse of her eyes. They were round and dark, glistening with unmistakable terror.

And then it came—that surge of pain from the past, intense and gripping, followed by the perfect photographic images I had stored away. There I was, lying in the doctor's office, my body swollen with the final weeks of pregnancy. The stethoscope was cold, but soon it warmed as the doctor moved it quietly in search of a heartbeat.

"Please hear it," I prayed.

The doctor reached up and turned off the music.

"No!" I screamed inside. "Hear the heartbeat above the music!" But there was nothing to hear.

The memory passed but not the pain as I slid the shovel carefully under the sterile eggs and laid them in the freshly dug hole. My daughter tried to keep Henrietta away from me, but it was useless. Feathers, leaves, and grass swirled low to the ground as Henrietta's wings beat helplessly to stop what she did not understand. I heard Millicent quacking from the daisies. She sat firm despite the commotion. I stopped.

Over the quacking I remembered staring at the pale blue flowers on Aunt Goldie's hat as she patted my huge front.

"I just know everything with be all right *this* time," she smiled, referring to my previous baby which had died days before her birth. I couldn't form the words to tell her that our baby was already dead. It was Christmas, after all.

I left the nest intact. Somehow I wanted to comfort Henrietta. It seemed a ridiculous notion. Henrietta was only a duck, but I knew we both had the same God-given instinct for nesting.

My daughter chased Millicent away from her nest. Henrietta poked her bill through the soft feathers, leaves, and grass searching in vain for her eggs. I headed toward the daisies and did what I had to do quickly amid frantic quacking from Millicent.

I found myself weeping. Through my tears, I saw two daisy buds lying on the ground. They had been accidentally cut down by my shovel. I knelt down and held them in my hands. They were so like my babies and so like the duck eggs—all tragically lost before they could live. I was left with only the pain and the picture perfect memories attached to it. I had no lock of hair or inked footprint. Nothing. But my pain was real. It was tangible evidence of my babies' lives. And for just a moment, I was grateful.

Crossing the Finish Line

ART E. BERG

After an accident that left me a quadriplegic,] the doctors took me into a separate room and explained to me that there were different terrains in life—hills, concrete, gravel, carpeting. They told me that because of the strength needed to push a manual wheelchair— strength which I would never have—in order to get around at all in life I would need an electric wheelchair. But I had a fear of the electric wheelchair. I feared that if I got used to the ease and convenience of just pushing a button to attain what I desired, my strength, enthusiasm, and self-esteem would slowly deteriorate.

Now came the problem of convincing the staff what I felt was best for me. When I first mentioned my feelings they resisted strongly, concerned for my new future. "You must use an electric wheelchair, Art. To get around this hospital on smooth linoleum floors is one thing, but for you to challenge the world without the use of a motor is not feasible. You'll need an electric chair."

"You don't understand," I replied. "I do not want an

electric wheelchair. I won't use it. I want a manual chair."

Finally they consented to consider my proposal if I could pass a test of my strength and ability. On the first floor of the hospital a track had been laid out measuring one-eighth of a mile. If I could push that distance in less than thirty minutes, I could have my manual wheelchair.

The morning of the event arrived. Doctors and nurses all stood around—anxious to see if I could finish—with a stopwatch to mark my progress. A piece of tape was stretched across the floor in front of me to signify the starting and finish line. Finally they clicked the watch and said, "Go!"

The first hallway was relatively easy as I made my way slowly down toward the end. By the time I reached the end of that first hallway, however, I was wondering whether I had made a wrong turn; my arms and shoulders began to tire and I began to question whether I would finish. In a state of exhaustion I made my way down the second hallway, the third, and finally the last, then crossed over that finish line—all in exactly twenty-eight minutes. So I got my manual wheelchair. . . .

When I went back to the hospital about a year and a half after I had left it, I decided to try that indoor track just one more time—the one that had previously taken twenty-eight minutes. This time there was nobody there except me—no doctors, nurses, or therapists . . . to encourage me. The tape was still on the floor, cracked and yellowing. Using the second hand on my watch to time me, I took off. Exactly one minute and fifty-eight seconds later I crossed that line again! Tears rolled down my cheeks as I reflected back over the months and years of effort, prayers, faith, and struggle which had been expended to reach this simple point in time and experience. I could not have felt more happy. Some people would not call that a miracle, but I do. And for the first time in my life I learned that dreams are never destroyed by circumstances. Dreams are born in the heart and in the mind, and only there can they ever die.

What God Hath Promised

ANNIE JOHNSON FLINT

God hath not promised
Skies always blue,
Flower-strewn pathways
All our lives through;
God hath not promised
Sun without rain,
Joy without sorrow,
Peace without pain.

But God hath promised
Strength for the day,
Rest for the labor,
Light for the way,
Grace for the trials,
Help from above,
Unfailing sympathy,
Undying love.

Hope Despite Holocaust

LLOYD D. NEWELL

*T*he faith-promoting story of Alice Alder, a Jew who survived the Holocaust, is sure to awaken . . . a God-fearing trust. Much like the more celebrated story of Victor Frankl (the Jewish prisoner who "thought" himself through the grueling captivity of a Nazi death camp and then told his stirring tale in his book *Man's Search for Meaning*), Alice Alder looked to God for physical, mental, and spiritual salvation. A thirty-one-year-old clothes designer and boutique owner in Hungary, Alice was enjoying a comfortable life-style when the Nazis invaded her homeland in 1944. Thrust from her thriving business and pleasant surroundings, she—along with many other Hungarian Jews—was forced into slave labor and moved from one concentration camp to another. Finally, she was put on a train bound for the gas chamber and the crematorium. An unquenchable belief that God had a purpose for her, however, gave Alice the necessary courage to leap from the train during a moment of welcome confusion—and save her life.

Injured, starving, and almost naked, Alice fought to survive in a strange land under uncertain circumstances. Eventually, a French partisan found her in this destitute condition and gave her the needed food and clothing to make a new start. Alice Alder looks back on that dark time through the illuminating lens of gratitude. She recognized then and glories now in the saving faith that carried her through: "I have always believed the hand of God was leading me. . . . I believe that somehow, somewhere, optimism and freedom will triumph." Alice made a divine connection that enabled her to see beyond the confines of her captivity and into the freedoms of a God-centered life. She believed in her ability to accomplish the "impossible," because she knew that God had purpose for her and would help her to live up to her greatest possibilities.

The Integrity of the Heart

A Daughter's Testimony

SCOTT ANDERSON

$\mathcal{D}$enice sat quietly in the back of the room. She seemed reluctant to leave. She kept feeling the prompting, and she felt she knew what she needed to do. But could she do it? She knew that Joseph Smith had found the courage to think of his mother's needs, and she understood that Nephi had found the courage, even when his father, Lehi, was murmuring, to go to his father for counsel. But her father was so far away from the Church and so disinterested. However, as she had listened that day in class to the account of the broken bow (see 1 Nephi 16) and listened as Lehi complained against God, and Nephi went to him *anyway,* the Spirit had plainly prompted her to reach out of her comfort zone and try to help her father. She was so busy in school and had so many other things to do, but she knew that in this time of her own great need, she should think of her father and try to find some way to help him. That night she prayed for strength to talk to her dad about the gospel. She was afraid of how he might respond, but she picked up the phone anyway to call him in Canada. In their conversation, she finally found the courage to try. "Dad, thank you for caring about me so much. I just want you to know how much I love you. You are one of the people I trust deeply in my life. I am learning some wonderful things here at school. Some of them are about the Book of Mormon and the Church, and I would like to share them with you—"

Her father interrupted the conversation. "Denice, you know how I feel about that—let's talk about something else."

"But, Dad, I've always felt that it would be wonderful if I could have a blessing from you, since no one loves me like you do."

"Let's talk about something else!" he snapped. Their brief conversation ended and left her feeling frustrated and empty.

Three months later, after enjoying many more wonderful experiences with the scriptures, Denice was headed home for Christmas. She called her father the night before she was to leave. In their conversation she couldn't hold back and once again she asked, "Dad, while I am home for the Christmas break, can I share some of the things I have been learning about the Church?"

"You know how I feel about that," came her father's terse reply. She didn't know what to say. Then the silence was broken by her father's tearful confession. "I'm sorry Denice, I just can't wait until you get home to tell you. When you talked to me last September, it touched me so deeply, I went to see the bishop the next day. I finished project temple about two weeks ago, and last week I was ordained an elder. I have a present wrapped under the tree that is an offer to give you a father's blessing while you are home. Thank you, Denice. Thank you for wanting so much to share all this with me."

The Few

EDGAR A. GUEST

The easy roads are crowded
And the level roads are jammed;
The pleasant little rivers
With the drifting folks are crammed.
But off yonder where it's rocky,
Where you get a better view,
You will find the ranks are thinning
And the travelers are few.

Where the going's smooth and pleasant
You will always find the throng,
For the many, more's the pity,
Seem to like to drift along.
But the steeps that call for courage,
And the task that's hard to do,
In the end result in glory
For the never-wavering few.

A Trip to the Temple

MARY ELLEN EDMUNDS

*O*ne day in our branch in Central Java, Indonesia, a wonderful member named Ibu Moelyono came to me with excitement, saying, "We have set a goal!" This surprised me, because it's not easy to set goals in developing areas. Life pretty much dictates what you will do and when, and few people have much money.

But I asked with enthusiasm, "What is your goal?" She said, "We're going to the temple!" Once again it caught me off guard. I knew that the average annual income for these friends in our branch would amount to about $150 in U.S. currency. I knew that the closest temple at the time was in Japan. I didn't know what to say, so I didn't say anything. Wise choice.

"Oh, Sister, we have figured out that if we sell everything in our home we don't need [and I'd been to their home, and I pictured it in my mind and wondered what on earth they had to sell], and if we save every Rupiah we possibly can, we'll be able to go in *fifty-five years.*"

By then I had kind of a lump in my throat, and I

continued to keep quiet, fighting the tears a bit. Then she added, "Oh, Sister, I hope we'll still be alive—we'll be 110!"

Elizabeth Francis Yates

CHIEKO N. OKAZAKI

$\mathscr{S}$ometimes we think of courage as occurring only in public arenas. The story of Elizabeth Francis Yates (the mother of Louise Yates Robison, the seventh general president of the Relief Society) shows a less public view. Elizabeth was an unlikely candidate for unconventional action. She had never lived or worked on her own. Raised in a cultured home in England with many comforts and strict training but no freedom and a limited, "genteel" education, she married at age fifteen. Within a few years she was the mother of four daughters. She matched the Victorian ideal of women as refined, pious, always gentle, and submissive. She did not care for her own religion, she says, but "it was very respectable, at least." However, she was too polite to refuse a Mormon missionary tract when it was offered, and on a rainy afternoon began reading it. Soon she was absorbed in the account of a debate between Elder John Taylor and some French ministers.

"When I had read it all," she wrote, "I said aloud, 'Praise the Lord. I have found the right way at last.'" She attended a meeting where Joseph Smith's mission was explained. "To say that I was thrilled with joy but feebly expresses my feelings at that time," she continues. "I could see no other way but to repent of my sins and to be baptized. I knew my people would bitterly oppose it when they knew it, and that my former friends would treat me coldly but it was worse than I ever thought."

That one sentence, "It was worse than I ever thought," contains an agony of heartbreak. Her mother forbade her to reenter her childhood home. Her husband told her she must choose between her family and her faith; weeping in anguish, she refused to deny her testimony, and he abandoned her and their four little girls. Elizabeth found work in a woolen mill, laboring with the baby in a basket by the loom, and managed to support them all. Seeing her undefeated, William returned and took all four children to London. Under the law then, there was nothing she could do to stop him or reclaim them.

She did not falter. Her last moment of hesitation had come on the very brink of her baptism when she looked down into the dark river at midnight, December 4, 1855. (The ceremony was performed in secret because of the risk of persecution.) She wrote, "[I] felt as though I could not possibly go in it, But a Voice seemed to say 'There is no other way.'" In faith, she took that step. "It seemed after that," she wrote, "that every thing had changed. The scales had fallen from my eyes, and the gospel plan was glorious, and I covenanted with My heavenly Father that however dark the clouds may be, if friends turned to be foes that by His help I would serve

Him. And I have tried in my faltering way to do so" (Lavina Fielding Anderson, "Elizabeth Francis Yates: Trial by Heartbreak," *Ensign,* July 1979, 62–63).

This story has a happy ending. Elizabeth reached Utah, married Thomas Yates, who loved her with all his heart, and had five more children. Two of the children in England died, but seven-year-old Susan ran away from her father when she was eleven, sought refuge with a Mormon family, and eventually was reunited with her mother in Utah. The father took the last daughter to the ends of the earth, he thought—Michigan—but Susan found her years later through a newspaper advertisement. All four daughters were sealed to Elizabeth and Thomas.

"With Eyes Now Blazing"

JOHN A. WIDTSOE

$\mathcal{T}$he three years after the autumn of 1894 were happy ones. . . .

During this time, as always, [Anna Widtsoe] was firm in her devotion to the gospel. The eternal truth restored through the Prophet Joseph Smith was the joy of her life. That faith she knew must be kept untarnished. That must be defended at all costs. She was everywhere the upholder of the Church, its principles and officers. At times this attitude was put to the test. For example:

About 1896, Moses Thatcher, an apostle of the Church, was suspended from service in the Quorum of the Twelve Apostles. Brother Thatcher, a man of unusual gifts and most charming personality, was very popular in his home town of Logan, as throughout the Church. His suspension caused widespread discussion, and many of his intimate Logan friends felt that he had been treated unjustly, and took his side against the action of the authorities of the Church. The temporary upheaval was tempestuous. Men's feelings ran high. While the excitement was at its height, two of the ward elders called at the Widtsoe home as ward teachers. [Anna, who was widowed, and her] two sons were home, and the whole family assembled to be instructed by the visiting teachers. Soon the visitors began to comment on the "Thatcher episode," as it was called, and explained how unjustly Brother Thatcher had been treated. [Anna] answered not a word, but there was a gathering storm in her stern eyes and high-held head.

After some minutes of listening to the visitors find fault with the Quorum of the Apostles with respect to Brother Thatcher, she slowly rose from her chair and as slowly walked to the entrance door of the house, which she threw wide open. With eyes now blazing she turned to the two brethren and said: "There is the door. I want you to leave this house instantly. I will not permit anyone in this house to revile the authorities of the Church, men laboring under divine inspiration. Nor do I wish such things spoken before my sons whom I have taught to love the leaders of the Church. And don't come back until you come in the right spirit to teach us the gospel. Here is the door. Now, go!" The visitors hurried out shamefacedly, for the widow had chastised them thoroughly. In defense of the gospel, Sister Widtsoe knew no fear.

"I Must Join the Church"

MARVIN J. ASHTON

*I*n the mission field I once met a young woman who had been a member of the Church for three years and who had been serving as a full-time missionary for three months. "How is your missionary life going?" I asked. "Quite well," she said. I could tell by her tone that perhaps she wanted to say more, so I said, "Share with me. Why do you report 'quite well' instead of 'very well'?" She replied, "Sometimes my heart aches when I look back and realize what a decisive choice I had to make." When I probed further, she told me this story:

"I had to make a choice between membership in The Church of Jesus Christ of Latter-day Saints and my mother's continuing love. My testimony and the conviction of my heart and mind told me the Church was true and that I must accept it. When I went to my mother and shared with her my desires and feelings, she told me, 'If you join the Mormon Church, just remember you don't have a mother anymore.' Elder Ashton, it was not easy for me to say to my mother, 'I must join the

Church. It is true, and I cannot deny it. I hope, Mother, that this will not be your decision, but if I must choose, I must choose the Church.'" Then she concluded, "It is not a pleasant and happy situation to be without a mother, but I know that with God's help I will win her back."

Not many of us must choose between church and parents. We have to admire a person who not only has joined the Church, accepted it fully, and is now sharing with others, but who also has the courage, after having made this important choice, to say, "I know that with God's help I will win my mother back."

Inside the Front Cover

HEIDI S. SWINTON

*W*hen ward mission leader Victor Brown donated a copy of the Book of Mormon to the public library in Hamilton, Ontario, Canada, it was an act of faith. He hoped that people would read the book and be converted. Three times he returned to the library to update his address and phone number on the sheet he had carefully placed in the front with the bold notation, "For more information." That was thirty years before, and not one person had called.

And then Kenneth Evans, seeking to find truths about life and death, checked out the Book of Mormon from the Hamilton library. He read it that night and all the next day. He called Victor Brown.

Kenneth and his wife had been sincerely searching for several years. . . .

Kenneth had always been interested in the ancient ruins of Mexico and Central and South America. He and an associate at work, Ray, had often talked of the mysteries and splendor of those civilizations. Ray mentioned that while he had been living in England, he had heard from two young men in a series of discussions the unbelievable story of a young man named Joseph Smith who had dug up a book about the ancient ruins and the societies that had built them. The missionaries had not interested Ray in the Church, but he did remember that the book was called the Book of Mormon.

That week the Evans family visited the public library, where Kenneth searched the files for the Book of Mormon. It was not listed. But by looking for works relating to "Mormons," he found *What of the Mormons?* by Gordon B. Hinckley, and he checked it out. He read the book that night and announced to his family, "This sounds like just the church we've been looking for! Now, we need to find a Book of Mormon."

They checked with the local bookstore only to be told rather curtly that they carried no such book. That Saturday Kenneth called the main public library downtown and asked the clerk to check the listings for a copy of the Book of Mormon. There was one. Kenneth asked her to hold it for him; he'd be right there.

He and his wife read the book all day and into the evening. They were interested in all they read. Maybe this was what they were seeking!

Inside the front cover of the book, a typed page fastened there by a Victor Brown gave a date thirty years old. In case more information was desired, Victor Brown had returned to the library to change his address and telephone number after each of three moves over the years. But he had moved a fourth time, and he hadn't made it back to make that change.

When Kenneth tried calling the last number listed, he

found no one there by the name of Brown. The phone book listed several pages of Browns but no Victor and only one with the initial "V"—a V.E.F. Brown.

He called.

Kenneth abruptly opened the conversation with, "I'd like you to tell me more about your church." Victor Brown thought someone, maybe another ward member, was playing a practical joke. But when Kenneth mentioned the book in the library, Brother Brown recognized the questioner was absolutely sincere.

"I know it's true. I know it's true," Brother Brown answered his caller in a voice full of emotion. Alice Brown, overhearing her husband's conversation, whispered to him, "Invite them to the Missionary Open House this Saturday."

The Evans family came. Many people were milling about between the booths and exhibits, watching the filmstrips and talking in groups. Kenneth and his family felt inconspicuous and comfortable among so many people who, too, showed interest. The Evanses didn't know they were the only investigators in attendance. And their hearts were touched. Their youngest son pleaded with his parents to come back to this place that felt so good.

The elders began visiting [the Evans'] home and teaching them the discussions. Friends, including their former pastor, cautioned them about involvement with the Mormons. But to no avail. On Christmas night, 1967, the Evans family was baptized. "What better way to honor him on this day when we celebrate his birth," their daughter Christine wrote of that poignant memory.

And in gratitude she added, "I often think of Brother Brown, who found his calling as a district missionary challenging but who followed a prompting of the Spirit to place that Book of Mormon in the library, where it waited all those years to be discovered. I think, too, of the missionaries in England, many years ago, who must have spent long hours teaching Ray all those discussions and of how discouraged they must have been when he still rejected their message. Yet he retained just enough knowledge of the Book of Mormon to be the spark my father needed to find out more."

Prisoners No More

BYUNG SIK HONG

Editor's Note: This story was told to Lloyd N. Andersen in Ogden, Utah, when Byung Sik Hong visited the USA and received his endowments in the Salt Lake Temple.

$\mathscr{B}$yung Sik Hong of Seoul, Korea, attended his first Church meeting at a U.S. military base where several hundred uniformed Mormons nearly wrung his hand off in their characteristic welcome of a native investigator. After his baptism, Hong sought every opportunity to tell his countrymen of his newfound faith. When he ran unsuccessfully for office in the Korean parliament, he even listed on his campaign posters "I am an elder of The Church of Jesus Christ of Latter-day Saints" as one of his qualifications as a candidate.

Upon completion of his studies at Seoul University, he was conscripted into the military, as was common at the time. As a result of a confrontation with a superior officer over a matter that he felt involved his conscience, Hong was confined several weeks in a military jail. He soon discovered that his cellmates viewed religion and the religious with great disdain. With considerable courage, he announced that he was both a Christian and a Mormon.

The cell in which Hong and his fellow military prisoners were held had been furnished, by a Christian Missionary Society, with a copy of the Holy Bible. Several of the prisoners tore pages from the Bible, rolled tobacco in them, stuck them into the corners of their mouths, lit them, and said, as they blew their smoke in Hong's face, "So you're a Mormon, are you? Well, let's talk about your religion."

So Hong talked about his religion. For days, the gospel of Jesus Christ occupied the hours of confinement in that spartan cell. The remaining pages of the Bible were flipped back and forth and passed from hand to hand as Hong explained his convictions. What a curious thing it was, a few weeks later, for two tall American missionaries to stoop their way into this same cell to interview several prisoners who had expressed the desire to be baptized. The interviews revealed that they were completely worthy for baptism. And even more curious was the scene a few days later when, with the permission of the military authorities, the missionaries took their "prisoners" down to the ocean under guard and baptized them.

God Grant Me This

EDGAR A. GUEST

God grant me this: the right to come at night
Back to my loved ones, head erect and true;
Beaten and bruised and from a losing fight,
Let me be proud in what I've tried to do.
Let me come home defeated if I must,
But clean of hands, and honor unimpaired,
Still holding firmly to my children's trust,
Still worthy of the faith which they have shared.
God grant me this: what e'er the fates decree,
Or do I win or lose life's little game,
I still would keep my children proud of me,
Nor once regret that they must bear my name.

Fresh Courage
Take . . .
All Is Well

"We Have Come Here to Kill Joe Smith"

LUCY MACK SMITH

$\mathcal{J}$oseph was at our house writing a letter. While he was thus engaged, I stepped to the door, and looking towards the prairie, I beheld a large company of armed men advancing towards the city, but, as I supposed it to be training day, said nothing about it.

Presently the main body came to a halt. The officers dismounting, eight of them came into the house. Thinking they had come for some refreshment, I offered them chairs, but they refused to be seated, and, placing themselves in a line across the floor, continued standing. I again requested them to sit, but they replied, "We do not choose to sit down; we have come here to kill Joe Smith and all the 'Mormons.'"

"Ah," said I, "what has Joseph Smith done, that you should want to kill him?"

"He has killed seven men in Daviess County," replied the foremost, "and we have come to kill him, and all his church."

"He has not been in Daviess County," I answered,

"consequently the report must be false. Furthermore, if you should see him, you would not want to kill him."

"There is no doubt that the report is perfectly correct," rejoined the officer; "it came straight to us, and I believe it; and we were sent to kill the Prophet and all who believe in him, and I'll be d——d if I don't execute my orders."

"I suppose," said I, "you intend to kill me, with the rest?"

"Yes, we do," returned the officer.

"Very well," I continued, "I want you to act the gentleman about it, and do the job quick. Just shoot me down at once, then I shall be at rest; but I should not like to be murdered by inches."

"There it is again," said he. "You tell a 'Mormon' that you will kill him, and they will always tell you, 'That is nothing—if you kill us, we shall be happy.'"

Joseph just at this moment finished his letter, and, seeing that he was at liberty, I said, "Gentlemen, suffer me to make you acquainted with Joseph Smith, the Prophet." They stared at him as if he were a spectre. He smiled, and stepping towards them, gave each of them his hand, in a manner which convinced them that he was neither a guilty criminal nor yet a hypocrite.

Joseph then sat down and explained to them the views, feelings, etc., of the Church, and what their course had been; besides the treatment which they had received from their enemies since the first. He also argued, that if any of the brethren had broken the laws, they ought to be tried by the law, before anyone else was molested. After talking with them some time in this way, he said, "Mother, I believe I will go home now—Emma will be expecting me." At this two of the men sprang to their feet, and declared that he should not go alone, as it would be unsafe—that they would go with him, in order to protect him. Accordingly the three left together.

And Thus History
Was Made

NICHOLAS G. MORGAN

$\mathcal{T}$he persecutions and violence through which
the Latter-day Saints were required to go in the early
days of the Church, especially during that period in
which they resided in Missouri, and Nauvoo, Illinois,
resulted in the development of men and women of great
faith and outstanding leadership.

Among that remarkable group of men who early
became associated with the Prophet Joseph Smith in the
building up of the Church, was Orson Spencer, a graduate from Union College of New York City and the
Hamilton Literary and Theological College. He was a
New Englander by birth and was reared in a home of
refinement and culture. His wife, Catherine Curtis
Spencer, also came from excellent New England stock.
She, too, was a university graduate and trained for a life
of refinement and ease.

Orson Spencer had been educated for the ministry
and was successfully carrying on his labors as a Baptist
preacher when information concerning The Church of

Jesus Christ of Latter-day Saints, then recently organized, reached him and his wife. After a complete investigation, he did not hesitate in accepting the Gospel, and he immediately commenced his ministry, which, from the beginning, became a very important factor in the establishment and development of the restored Church of Jesus Christ.

When he gathered with the Saints in Nauvoo, he was completely cut off from association with his relatives and former friends. His wife's parents became so embittered that they refused her admission to their home, and advised her that they did not care to correspond further with her.

In Nauvoo, during the year 1846, the persecutions became so vicious and intolerable that Orson Spencer and his wife were in constant jeopardy. Like that of many other Mormon women, the health of Sister Spencer gradually became impaired, and her husband, fearing that she might not be able to stand the ordeals which he realized the Mormon people were about to be called to undergo, wrote to his wife's parents, asking that they take her back into their home, that she might convalesce, and until the Saints were situated where they could live in peace and harmony, away from the persecutions of the mobocrats.

He waited patiently for a favorable reply to this letter. None came, however, and eventually the time arrived when those living in Nauvoo were compelled to cross the Mississippi and journey westward to the new location, where the main body of the Church would be brought by its leaders.

It was in the month of March, 1846, when Orson Spencer and his wife crossed the river to Iowa, prepared, with their wagon and ox team, for the journey that lay before them. It was miserable weather. It rained almost daily, and occasionally sleet would fall or be blown by cold, wintry winds. The road, such as it was, was so muddy that at times the wheels would sink to the axles.

After leaving Nauvoo, Sister Spencer's health continued to get worse, and eventually she was confined to her bed in the covered wagon. It was on a night about five days after leaving Sugar Creek that she suddenly grew much worse. That night the storm increased in its severity. Little streams of water trickled through the holes in the canvas stretched over the wagon, and kind friends, who had come to Brother Spencer's aid, held milk pans over his sick wife to keep her from being drenched. Occasionally she would look out through the openings in the wagon covering and see the lightning leap across the midnight sky.

It was at about this time that a messenger on horseback brought the latest mail from Nauvoo. In it was a letter for Orson Spencer. Brother Spencer opened it and found it to be a communication from his wife's parents, in which they acknowledged the receipt of his letter, but refused to have further interest or care for their daughter unless, as they said in closing, "let her denounce her degrading faith, and she can come back, but never until she does."

Sister Spencer listened to the reading of the letter, but murmured not a word. As her husband completed the reading, she turned to him and in a very weak voice, caused by her illness, asked him to get his Bible and read to her from the sixteenth verse of the first chapter of Ruth. He complied with her request and read as follows:

"And Ruth said, Intreat me not to leave thee, or to return from following after thee: for whither thou goest, I will go; and where thou lodgest, I will lodge: thy people shall be my people, and thy God my God."

He ceased reading. A calm, peaceful smile spread over the lovely, refined face of his wife. Her eyelids drooped and closed in a sweet, peaceful sleep from which she was not to awake until the morning of the resurrection.

The next morning, amid the hustle and bustle of camp life, a grave was dug by the side of the road, and there on the Iowa prairie the last remains of a great and good woman were laid to rest. An hour later the caravan of covered wagons was again on the march westward.

History has not recorded, nor will there yet be recorded, the lives of men and women of greater faith, greater love, and greater devotion, than those of our Pioneer fathers and mothers who gave their all in the establishment of that which we now enjoy so much.

Hole in the Rock

BRENT L. TOP

$\mathcal{M}$any of [the] early pioneers arrived in the Salt Lake Valley after the arduous trek only to find that they were not done pioneering yet. Responding to the call of the prophet of God, many once again packed up their wagons and moved to the other frontier areas of the Great Basin to establish additional Mormon settlements. Joseph Stanford Smith was called to settle in the Colorado River basin. He had been one of the most active leaders in helping blaze a trail through a treacherous canyon in southern Utah that became known as "Hole-in-the-Rock." On January 26, 1880, Stanford spent the day helping all of the wagons in the company get down through the notch in the rocky canyon. Using ropes and pulleys as well as logs tied to the backs of wagons as a braking system, each wagon was carefully lowered through the rocky crevice and driven to the banks of the river and then ferried across. When word came that all of the wagons were safely down and across the river, Stanford looked for his wagon—but it was nowhere to be found. It was still up on top of the canyon. It had been moved back while the others were being taken down, and now it had been overlooked. His wife, Arabella, and his children were waiting for him at the top of the canyon.

"For a moment Stanford's face flushed with rage. He threw his hat on the ground and stomped it—as was his habit when he was angry.

"'With me down there helping get their wagons on the raft, I thought some one would bring my wagon down. Drat 'em!'

"'I've got the horses harnessed and things all packed,' Belle breathlessly assured him as they ran toward the wagon."

Stanford unlocked the brakes; checked the team; tied old Nig, the mule, to the back axle as a brake; and cross-locked the wheels with chains.

"They walked to the top of the crevice, where hand in hand they looked down—10 feet of loose sand, then a rocky pitch as steep as the roof of a house and barely as wide as the wagon—below that a dizzy chute down to the landing place. . . . It was that first drop of 150 feet that frightened him.

"'I am afraid we can't make it,' he exclaimed.

"'But we've got to make it,' she answered calmly. . . .

"'If we only had a few men to hold the wagon back we might make it, Belle.'

"'I'll do the holding back,' said Belle, 'on old Nig's lines.'"

She then busied herself getting the children to a safe place back from the crevice. Three-year-old Roy held the baby, and sister Ada sat in front of them and said a little prayer as Belle kissed each of them and tucked quilts snugly around them. "Don't move, dears. Don't even stand up. As soon as we get the wagon down, Papa will come back for you!"

"Stanford braced his legs against the dashboard and they started down through the Hole-in-the-Rock. The first lurch nearly pulled Belle off her feet. She dug her heels in to hold her balance. Old Nig was thrown to his haunches. Arabella raced after him and the wagon, holding to the lines with desperate strength. Nig rolled to his side and gave a shrill neigh of terror. . . .

"[Belle] lost her balance and went sprawling after old Nig. She was blinded by the sand which streamed after her. She gritted her teeth and hung on to the lines. A jagged rock tore her flesh and hot pain ran up her leg from heel to hip. The wagon struck a huge boulder. The impact jerked her to her feet and flung her against the side of the cliff."

The wagon stopped at the end of the chute. Stanford jumped off the wagon and first noticed the bloodied, bruised, and almost lifeless mule that had been dragged most of the way down. There, holding onto the reins, blood streaming from her leg, and covered from head to foot with dirt, was Arabella. She had been dragged down along with the mule—but she wouldn't let go. She had hung on for all she was worth. Miraculously they made it down and were safe.

"'Darling, will you be all right?'

"'Of course I will. Just leave me here and go as fast as you can for the children.'

"'I'll hurry,' he flung over his shoulder and began the steep climb up the incline they had just come down.

" . . . He slowed down, and looked around. He had driven a wagon down that fearful crevice, and dragged his wife behind. . . . God bless her gallant heart! He kicked the rocks at his feet and with tears streaming down his face lifted his hat in salute to Arabella, his wife" (as told by a grandson, Raymond Smith Jones, in David E. Miller, *Hole-in-the-Rock: An Epic in the Colonization of the Great American West* [Salt Lake City: University of Utah Press, 1966], 111–14).

President Harold B. Lee said, "We have some tight places to go before the Lord is through with this church and the world in this dispensation. . . . The power of Satan will increase; we see it in evidence on every hand (Conference Report, October 1970, 152).

Whether the "tight places" are *institutional* or *individual,* it will take faith and courage to hang on like Arabella Smith. . . . Christ is the iron rod to which we must cling—never loosening our grip, never letting go. Never. For if we will continually hang on to him, he will never let go of us. Never. No, not ever!

Crossing the Sweetwater

SOLOMON F. KIMBALL

$\mathcal{T}$o describe conditions surrounding the old fort at Devil's Gate during the first few days of November, 1856, would be a difficult task. About twenty-five out of the nine hundred emigrants who had arrived there since the [second] of the month, had already perished, and others were lying at the point of death. Their food supply was nearly exhausted, and there were no signs of help. The snow was eighteen inches deep on the level, and the weather intensely cold. Feed was scarce, and cattle were dying by the score. Wood was almost out of the question, and the more feeble among the Saints were literally freezing to death. Unless immediate steps were taken to relieve the situation, all would perish together.

Captain Grant, thoroughly conversant with these facts, ordered his men to make a start for the west in charge of the Martin company even if they accomplished no more than to find a better camping ground where wood and feed could be secured in greater abundance. Those of the handcart people who were unable to walk were crowded into the overloaded wagons, and a start was made; the balance of the company hobbling along behind with their carts as best they could.

When the boys came to the first crossing of the Sweetwater west of Devil's Gate, they found the stream full of floating ice, making it dangerous to cross, on account of the strong current. However, the teams went over in safety and continued on their way until they came to a sheltered place, afterwards called "Martin's Hollow." Here they camped for the night and, after burying a number of Saints who had died during the day, busied themselves in getting ready to receive the remainder of the company who were expected at any moment.

When the people who were drawing carts came to the brink of this treacherous stream, they refused to go any further, realizing what it meant to do so, as the water in places was almost waist deep, and the river more than a hundred feet wide by actual measurement. To cross that mountain torrent under such conditions to them meant nothing short of suicide, as it will be remembered that nearly one-sixth of their number had already perished from the effects of crossing North Platte, eighteen days before. They believed that no earthly power could bring them through that place alive, and reasoned that if they had to die it was useless to add to their suffering by the perpetration of such a rash act as crossing the river here. They had walked hundreds of miles over an almost trackless plain, pulling carts as they went, and after making such tremendous sacrifices for the cause of truth, to lay down their lives in such a dreadful manner was awful to contemplate. They became alarmed, and cried mightily unto the Lord for help, but received no answer. All the warring elements of nature appeared to be against them, and the spirit of death itself seemed to be in the very air.

After they had given up in despair, after all hopes had vanished, after every apparent avenue of escape seemed closed, three eighteen-year-old boys belonging to the relief party came to the rescue, and to the astonishment of all who saw, carried nearly every member of that ill-fated handcart company across the snowbound stream. The strain was so terrible, and the exposure so great, that in later years all the boys died from the effects of it. When President Brigham Young heard of this heroic act, he wept like a child, and later declared publicly, "that act alone will ensure C. Allen Huntington, George W. Grant and David P. Kimball an everlasting salvation in the Celestial Kingdom of God, worlds without end."

"To Become
Acquainted with God"

DAVID O. MCKAY

A teacher, conducting a class, said it was
unwise ever to attempt, even to permit [the Martin
handcart company] to come across the plains under
such conditions.

Some sharp criticism of the Church and its leaders
was being indulged in for permitting any company of
converts to venture across the plains with no more supplies or protection than a handcart caravan afforded.

An old man in the corner sat silent and listened as
long as he could stand it, then he arose and said things
that no person who heard him will ever forget. His face
was white with emotion, yet he spoke calmly, deliberately, but with great earnestness and sincerity.

In substance [he] said, "I ask you to stop this criticism. You are discussing a matter you know nothing
about. Cold historic facts mean nothing here, for they
give no proper interpretation of the questions involved.
Mistake to send the Handcart Company out so late in
the season? Yes. But I was in that company and my wife

was in it and Sister Nellie Unthank whom you have cited was there, too. We suffered beyond anything you can imagine and many died of exposure and starvation, but did you ever hear a survivor of that company utter a word of criticism? Not one of that company ever apostatized or left the Church, because everyone of us came through with the absolute knowledge that God lives for we became acquainted with him in our extremities.

"I have pulled my handcart when I was so weak and weary from illness and lack of food that I could hardly put one foot ahead of the other. I have looked ahead and seen a patch of sand or a hill slope and I have said, I can go only that far and there I must give up, for I cannot pull the load through it. . . . I have gone on to that sand and when I reached it, the cart began pushing me. I have looked back many times to see who was pushing my cart, but my eyes saw no one. I knew then that the angels of God were there.

"Was I sorry that I chose to come by handcart? No. Neither then nor any minute of my life since. The price we paid to become acquainted with God was a privilege to pay, and I am thankful that I was privileged to come in the Martin Handcart Company."

The Journey of the Julia Ann

KAREN LYNN DAVIDSON

In 1855, twenty-eight Latter-day Saint converts from Australia set sail, bound for Zion by way of San Francisco. Two of the passengers were returning American missionaries. An Australian couple, Andrew and Elizabeth Anderson, boarded the ship with their eight children. One young family, the Harrises, could not afford passage for both adults, so Eliza Harris traveled on ahead with her two-year-old and six-month-old children to join the Saints, with her husband planning to follow as soon as he could earn his fare. Martha Humphries and her three children sailed without their husband and father for the same reason. Also aboard were an equal number of non-Latter-day Saints, including the captain, an American, by the name of Benjamin Franklin Pond. As the voyage began, the Saints gathered to sing "The Gallant Ship Is under Weigh," a hymn written by William W. Phelps to cheer the hearts of the immigrants and missionaries who were a constant part of the early Latter-day Saint scene. . . .

After about a month at sea, the *Julia Ann* was in

rough waters about midway between Australia and Hawaii. At 8:30 in the evening, after most of the children were asleep, the ship smashed head-on into a coral reef.

Captain Pond saw at once that the ship was finished; the only question remaining was whether any lives could be saved in the terrible storm. Passengers tried to cling to the railing around the deck, but some of the younger children could not keep a handhold as the huge waves swept over them; little Marion Anderson and Mary Humphries were washed overboard and never seen again.

The *Julia Ann* did not sink; it began to break into pieces on the rocks with the continual crashing of the waves. Only one lifeboat remained, but it was unmanageable in the storm. At the request of Captain Pond, a crew member volunteered to leap over the side and swim to the reef—hardly an inviting refuge, rough, jagged and partially submerged in the pounding waves; he managed to fasten a rope to one of the rocks, so that passengers could use the rope as a hand-over-hand lifeline and leave the ship. One by one the women and children were urged to try this means of escape, but some could not bring themselves to step off into the empty black night above the swirling water.

Eliza Harris bravely strapped her six-month-old baby to her breast and prepared to make her way to the rocks, but at that moment a huge wave engulfed them. Both mother and baby son were drowned. A young mother [only seventeen years of age] managed to struggle to the rock, along with her husband who carried their baby strapped to his back. Another mother, urged by Captain Pond to save her own life since her six children could not possibly make it to the rocks, decided to remain on board rather than let her children face death alone. . . .

At last only nineteen passengers remained on the boat, all of them parents and children who had decided to face death together. The captain and the remaining crew members, knowing they had done all they could, made their way along the rope to the reef. Then, at about 11 P.M., the ship broke into pieces. Miraculously, the part of the ship to which the passengers were clinging was carried up onto the reef, and the remaining passengers were saved. In all, of the fifty-six who had originally sailed on the ship, fifty-one survived.

And so they waited on the reef for the dawn, all of them injured and exhausted, up to their waists in water, threatened constantly by sharks. Yes, they were alive, but what was to happen now? . . . They were miles away from the route of passing ships and entirely without a supply of drinking water.

When the sun rose, they saw an island about eight miles distant. Making some quick repairs to the remaining lifeboat, the captain and some crew members rowed to the island. In the meantime, some of those remaining on the reef managed to build a raft and salvage a few supplies from the shipwreck. But when the captain and his men returned that afternoon, they brought a discouraging report: the island was really only a sandbar, with apparently neither water nor food.

Even so, the sandbar was preferable to the coral reef, and the entire company was eventually transported there. Their spirits rose when they found that some shallow wells would yield drinking water. They discovered crabs and coconuts. . . .

Thus they lived for forty-seven days. They knew that their only chance for rescue lay in rowing the battered lifeboat for help. Either they had to take this gamble or resign themselves to remaining on the sandbar forever. So the captain and the crew set out. After four days of nonstop rowing, they reached the island of Bora-Bora. Captain Pond arranged for a rescue ship, and sixty days after the shipwreck the grateful passengers sighted the sails of the *Emma Packer,* sent to carry them to safety in Tahiti.

A Confirmation
at the Water's Edge
PRISCILLA MOGRIDGE STAINES

I was brought up in the Episcopal faith from my earliest childhood, my parents being members of the Episcopal Church. But as my mind became matured, and I thought more about religion, I became dissatisfied with the doctrines taught by that church, and I prayed to God my Heavenly Father to direct me aright, that I might know the true religion.

Shortly after being thus concerned about my salvation, I heard Mormonism and believed it. God had sent the true gospel to me in answer to my prayer.

It was a great trial for a young maiden (I was only nineteen years of age) to forsake all for the gospel—father, mother, brothers and sisters—and to leave my childhood home and native land, never expecting to see it again. This was the prospect before me. The Saints were already leaving the fatherland, in obedience to the doctrine of gathering, which was preached at this time with great plainness by the elders as an imperative command of God. We looked upon the gathering as necessary to our salvation. Nothing of our duty in this respect was concealed, and we were called upon to emigrate to America as soon as the way should open, to share the fate of the Saints, whatever might come. Young as I was and alone of all my family in the faith, I was called to take up my cross and lay my earthly all upon the altar; yet so well satisfied was I with my new religion that I was willing to make every sacrifice for it in order to gain my salvation and prove myself not unworthy of the Saints' reward.

Having determined to be baptized, I resolved to at once obey the gospel, although it was midwinter and the weather bitterly cold.

It is proper to here state that baptism was a trial to the converts in England in those days. They had to steal away, even unknown to their friends oftentimes, and scarcely daring to tell the Saints themselves that they were about to take up the cross; and not until the ordinance had been administered, and the Holy Ghost gave them boldness, could they bring themselves to proclaim openly that they had cast in their lot with the despised Mormons. Nor was this all, for generally the elders had to administer baptism when the village was wrapt in sleep, lest persecutors should gather a mob to disturb the solemn scene with gibes and curses, accompanied with stones or clods of earth torn from the river bank and hurled at the disciple and minister during the performance of the ceremony.

On the evening of a bitterly cold day in midwinter, as before stated, I walked four miles to the house of a local elder for baptism. Arriving at his house, we waited until midnight, in order that the neighbors might not disturb us, and then repaired to a stream of water a quarter of a mile away. Here we found the water, as we anticipated, frozen over, and the elder had to chop a hole in the ice large enough for the purpose of baptism. It was a scene and an occasion I shall never forget. Memory today brings back the emotions and sweet awe of that moment. None but God and his angels, and the few witnesses who stood on the bank with us, heard my covenant; but in the solemnity of that midnight hour it seemed as though all nature were listening, and the recording angel writing our words in the book of the Lord. Is it strange that such a scene, occurring in the life of a Latter-day Saint, should make an everlasting impression, as this did on mine?

Having been thus baptized, I returned to the house in my wet and freezing garments.

Up to this hour, as intimated, my heart's best affection had been centered on home, and my greatest mental struggle in obeying the gospel had been over the thought of soon leaving that home; but no sooner had I emerged from the water, on that night of baptism, and received my confirmation at the water's edge, than I became filled with an irresistible desire to join the Saints who were gathering to America.

The Lost Oxen of Mary Fielding Smith

DON C. CORBETT

*T*he Smith family] camped one evening on an open prairie on the Missouri River bottom by the side of a small spring creek which emptied into the river about three quarters of a mile from them. Where they were camped, they were in plain sight of the river and could apparently see over every foot of the little open prairie in the direction of the river to the southwest, the bluffs on the northwest, and the timber which skirted the prairie on the right and left.

Camping nearby on the other side of the creek were some men with a herd of beef cattle which they were driving to Savannah and St. Joseph for market. Joseph F. and his uncle usually unyoked their oxen and turned them loose to feed during their encampment at night, but this time, on account of the proximity of the herd of cattle, and fearing that they might get mixed up and be driven off, they turned the oxen out to feed in their yokes. The next morning when they came to look for them, to their great astonishment, their best yoke of oxen was not to be found.

Joseph F. and his Uncle Fielding spent all the morning and well nigh until noon hunting for them but to no avail. The grass was tall and in the morning wet with heavy dew. Tramping through this grass, through the woods, and over the bluff, made them wet to the skin, fatigued, disheartened, and almost exhausted.

In this pitiable plight, Joseph F. was the first to return to camp. As he approached, he saw his mother kneeling serenely in prayer. He halted a moment then drew gently near enough to hear her pleading with the Lord not to suffer them to be left in this helpless condition but to lead them to recover their lost team that they might continue their travel in safety.

When she arose from her knees, Joseph F. was standing nearby. The first expression that he caught upon her face was a lovely smile which gave him renewed hope and an assurance that he had not felt before.

A few moments later, Uncle Fielding returned to camp soaked with dew, faint, fatigued, and thoroughly disheartened. His first words were: "Well Mary, the cattle are gone!"

Mary replied in a voice which fairly rang with cheerfulness: "Never mind. Your breakfast has been waiting for hours and, now, while you and Joseph F. are eating, I will just take a walk out and see if I can find the cattle."

"Why Mary," he exclaimed, "what do you mean? We have been all over this country, all through the timber and through the herd of cattle, and our oxen are gone;

they are not to be found. I believe they have been driven off, and it is useless for you to attempt to do such a thing as to hunt for them."

"Never mind me," replied Mary, "get your breakfast and I will see."

She started toward the river, following down the spring creek. Before she was out of speaking distance, the man in charge of the herd of cattle rode up from the opposite side of the creek and called out: "Madam, I saw your oxen over in that direction this morning about daybreak," pointing in the opposite direction from that in which Mary was going.

Joseph Fielding and Joseph F. heard plainly what the man said, but Mary went right on and did not even turn her head to look at him. A moment later, the man rode off rapidly toward his herd which had been gathered in the opening near the edge of the woods. They were soon under full drive for the road leading toward Savannah, and quickly disappeared from view.

Mary continued straight down the little stream of water until she stood almost on the bank of the river, and then she beckoned toward the wagon. Joseph F. was watching his mother's every movement and was determined that she should not get out of his sight. Instantly, he and his uncle arose from the mess-chest, on which their breakfast had been spread, and started toward her. Joseph . . . outran his uncle and came first to the spot where his mother stood. There, he saw their oxen fastened to a clump of willows growing in the bottom by the little spring creek, perfectly concealed from view. They were not long in releasing them from bondage and getting them back to the camp, where all the other cattle had been tied to the wagon wheels all the morning. They were soon on their way rejoicing. The worthy herdsman had suddenly departed when he saw that Mary would not heed him.

This story of the lost oxen gives a deep insight into the makeup of Mary Smith. She was confronted with an awkward crisis in her life—a difficult situation which happened far from anywhere with no human to call upon for help. She did not panic but put perfect trust in the Lord to come to her rescue and help find the oxen. In the moment of alarm, she went to her knees and talked with Him and asked for assistance. She arose smiling and serene as if the spirit of the Lord had given her an immediate answer. Her instinct resisted the false and beguiling direction of the herdsman, knowing for certain that he could not be trusted. Then with resolute will, she walked unerringly to where her oxen were concealed. This was a clue, as the cowman quickly found out, to the kind of a woman she was. She revealed the kind of mind and faith that would triumph and take her to the mountains.

Healing the Oxen

DON C. CORBETT

*W*hen [Mary Fielding Smith's party] reached camp, Captain Lott showed dissatisfaction with Mary's efforts. He asked her how many wagons she had. She told him, seven, which probably included the two wagons of her brother. Lott then wanted to know how many yokes of oxen she had. Her answer was, four, plus a number of cows and calves. Then the Captain "lowered the boom." He told the widow that it was folly for her to start under such conditions. She would never make it and, if she started, she would be a burden upon the company the whole way. He advised her to go back to Winter Quarters and wait until she could get help.

Mary's son Joseph F. heard the Captain's remarks and resented them. He knew how Lott's words hurt his mother after her exhausting struggle to get ready. Had he been a bit older he would have spoken his mind to the Captain. The boy only bit his lip and walked away. After the Captain had had his say, Mary was silent for a moment—an all important moment—then she calmly told the Captain that she would beat him to the Valley and would ask no help from him. . . .

Things went along quite smoothly until they reached a point midway between the Platte and the Sweetwater rivers, when one of Mary's oxen lay down in the yoke as if poisoned and all supposed he would die. All the teams in the rear stopped, and many gathered around to see what had happened. In a short time, the Captain perceived that something was wrong and came to the spot. The ox stiffened in the throes of death. The Captain blustered about and exclaimed: "'He is dead, there is no use working with him, we'll have to fix up some way to take the Widow along. I told her she would be a burden on the company.'" But in this, he was greatly mistaken.

Mary said nothing but went to her wagon and returned with a bottle of consecrated oil. She asked her brother Joseph and James Lawson to administer to her fallen ox, believing that the Lord would raise him. It was a solemn moment there under the open sky. A hush fell over the scene. The men removed their hats. All bowed their heads as Joseph Fielding, who had been promised by Heber C. Kimball that he would have power to raise the dead, knelt, laid his hands on the head of the prostrate ox, and prayed over it. The great beast lay stretched out and very still. Its glassy eyes looked nowhere. A moment after the administration the animal stirred. Its huge, hind legs commenced to gather under it. Its haunches started to rise. The forelegs strengthened. The ox stood and, without urging, started off as if nothing had happened. This amazing thing greatly astonished the onlookers.

They hadn't gone very far when another ox "Old Bully," lay down under exactly the same circumstances. This time it was one of her best oxen, the loss of which would have been very serious. Again, the holy ordinance was administered, with the same results.

An Unexpected Visitor

CLARISSA YOUNG SPENCER

The first house to be built outside of the fort in Salt Lake City was the home of Father's brother, Lorenzo D. Young. It was built in the fall of 1847, just two or three months after the arrival of the first company of pioneers, and stood upon the present site of the Beehive House.

The Youngs moved into this small dwelling—about one-half mile away from the protection of the fort—very much against the advice and wishes of their friends, and it so happened that the catastrophe predicted for them was almost realized. While Uncle Lorenzo was working away from the house one day, leaving his wife and young baby alone, a tall Indian appeared and demanded bread. The mother had only three small biscuits in the house, and of these she gave the [Indian] two. He was not satisfied and demanded more. She gave him the last one, but he still insisted upon more. She told him that she had no more, whereupon he became furious and, fitting an arrow to his bow, took aim at her heart. This pioneer woman was not only courageous—she was also

175

resourceful. Making as if she were going to comply with his demand, she went into the next room and untied a large mastiff. "Seize him," she called in a low voice, and with a bound the dog had sprung at the Indian's throat and thrown him to the floor.

The Indian pleaded for his life, and after taking the precaution to remove his bow and arrow, she called off the dog. The Indian was badly hurt, and Aunt Harriet, matching her courage with kindness, bathed and dressed the wound and sent him away, a sadder and wiser Indian.

God Our
Strength Will Be

The "Shepard" Who Led Astray

KRIS MACKAY

$\mathcal{S}$ECRETS OF THE MORMON TEMPLE EXPOSED!

Those words fairly jumped at Elder Rulon Killian. He was a missionary at a time when Mormon standards and ethics were not widely known [1924], and missionary work required all the faith and courage a young man had to give. . . .

The eye-catching words were printed on placards and tacked to utility poles throughout the city. They appeared in big, black, bold print under pictures of handsome, silver-haired Mrs. Lula Loveland Shepard, newly arrived in Chattanooga, Tennessee, for a series of lectures on the subject. . . .

She spoke that night in one of the largest, most fashionable churches in town. The hall was packed, with standing room at a premium, and disappointed people turned away at the door. [Elder Killian] managed to slip in and mingle inconspicuously in a rear corner.

With her on the stand sat many of the city's prominent

ministers. One offered a solemn prayer in her behalf. Sacred songs were sung. Then Mrs. Shepard rose to hold her audience spellbound with one fabricated and infamous story after another. . . .

She said, "Few realize what a menace we have facing the safety of our nation. I recently had an audience with President Warren G. Harding. I suggested he send an army and break down the doors of that wicked temple and put an end to this curse, once and for all. He agreed with me. He said, 'Mrs. Shepard, I will appoint you my personal agent to go throughout this country and muster the support I'll need.'

"Now, folks," she persuaded, "that's exactly why I'm here. But it costs money. Lots of money. Ushers will pass among you and accept donations. Please be generous."

. . . She wasn't through yet. "I have just been informed," she continued shrilly, "that Mormon elders work right here in Chattanooga and hold street meetings each Saturday evening on the corner of Main and Market. Tomorrow is Saturday! How many will go with me to that corner at seven o'clock? Of course, they are all cowards, and they will hear of our coming and won't show up. But who will be with me in case they do?"

Every hand in the room shot up without hesitation— including Elder Killian's. Good sense whispered it wasn't prudent to have his identity questioned at that point.

He didn't get much sleep that night. . . . A modern civil war raged in his mind all that night and the following day. The left side of him said, "You are a fool if you try to hold a meeting. That mob will tear you to shreds." . . .

But the right side held the clincher: "God will protect you."

He climbed on the streetcar and was sorely tempted to climb off again a dozen times before it reached Main and Market streets. The streetcar rounded the corner, and when he saw the restless, gathering crowd, courage failed him completely and he rode on.

His left side was exultant. "I'm glad you got smart. There have been two elders murdered in Tennessee already [Elders Gibbs and Berry], and you will be the third as sure as you leave this car." And he didn't leave it—not for two more blocks.

Then his right side got the upper hand. It ordered, calmly and positively, "Get out! You are going to hold that street meeting, murder or no murder."

With that side in control and with courage strong, at least for the moment, he jumped off and ran swiftly back to the appropriate corner. He elbowed his way roughly to the center of the crowd, tossed his hat down on the curb with a flourish, threw back his head, and sang one rousing verse of "High on the Mountain Top." The intersection was jammed, and traffic completely stalled. People pressed in around him until he could hardly move. Next he bowed his head for a short, vocal prayer. Then he said loudly, "My friends, I'm glad to be here tonight."

That did it. That was as far as he got. The spell of stunned indecision at his audacity was broken.

Like waves during a hurricane they moved in upon

him from all sides, the roar of their outrage swelling as they came. They reached out for him—and a sudden, solid, blinding sheet of rain changed their minds.

What a deluge! It didn't rain individual drops; it came down by bucketfuls and grew worse by the second. This was no ordinary storm. Within seconds the aroused mob was soaked to the skin, as wet as if they had fallen into a river. Women screamed hysterically, men shrieked, and all scampered for open doorways or out-stretched awnings.

In the confusion, Elder Killian was forgotten. The storm continued unabated until the streets were empty and he was alone. He boarded a passing street car and returned to his room. He was dazed by the suddenness of it all and by the natural means the Lord had employed to save him from a crowd stirred to mob frenzy by a clever, polished tool of the devil. He knelt and thanked his heavenly Father that his courage had not failed.

Early next morning he received a telegram from Mission President Charles A. Callis. It read, "Elder Killian, I just learned Mrs. Shepard is in Chattanooga, and you are laboring there alone. Get out of town and don't return until that 'infernal female' has left."

He didn't have to be coaxed. He was aboard the next train, speeding gratefully toward safety.

Splits with Elder Begay

RANDAL A. WRIGHT

$\mathscr{S}$everal years ago when I was serving as a stake missionary, I was privileged to meet a full-time missionary from Utah named Maurice Begay. Elder Begay was a full-blooded Indian and a perfect example of one who had "blossomed as a rose."

He showed me, during a "missionary split" one night, why we sometimes need to let our lights shine, even when it's hard. That night as we were out tracting, we drove into a poor area of town. Elder Begay asked me to pull up to a particular mobile home so we could tract it out. I tried to tell him that I was sure the people who lived there would not be interested in the Church, but he would not listen and began to walk up the driveway. I followed him past a couple of junked cars and scattered trash up to the trailer door. I was more than a little nervous as Elder Begay knocked loudly on the door. My confidence sank even more when the man of the house opened the door. He had a cigarette in his mouth, no shirt, tattoos all over his arms, and a scowl on his face. "What do you want?" he asked. I thought, "I want to go home. What do you think I want?" But I said nothing. Elder Begay told him who we were and asked if we could come in and share a message about Christ's visit to the Americas with his family.

After a long pause, he invited us in. In his small living room sat his wife and four children. All needed a comb, a bath, a handkerchief, and some better clothing. There was tension in the air as we sat down, and it became obvious that no one was going to speak to us because of their involvement in a TV movie. After a short time, Elder Begay told the family we had a message to share with them. No one responded to his comment. I became more nervous and had a strong desire to get up and leave.

The elder tried two more times to talk with the family about the Church, but still they would not reply. After we had sat there for about fifteen minutes, Elder Begay did something that took as much courage as anything I have ever seen. With no warning this young missionary picked up his chair and set it right in front of the TV set, then sat down so the family could not see the movie. Then he reached around and turned off the set. "You don't mind if I turn this off do you?" he asked. There was an eery silence in the room as the family stared at him in disbelief. I have never wanted to run so bad in all my life. After what seemed like an eternity, the man replied, "I guess not; I've already seen that movie anyway." Hearing that brought me more relief that I can describe.

That night a young Lamanite missionary taught that family about Joseph Smith and the Restoration. The family was not interested in the Church, just as I had first suspected, but I had witnessed one of the most inspirational events of my life.

"This Is Where I Am Supposed to Be"

KATHRYN SCHLENDORF

*M*om! I'm really doing this!" My daughter was starting to hyperventilate in the backseat of the car. We were on our way to the Missionary Training Center. She had five suitcases full of an eighteen-month supply of everything a girl could imagine needing. A huge quilt was tied to her pillow, and hangers were tied onto that. All the MTC officials stared at the haul as it came through the doors. She would walk through one door, and with that step her childhood would be over; parental nurturing would be suspended; memories of lazy Saturday mornings and late-night adventures with friends would be packed in boxes with all her possessions, and left in the storage room until she returned.

What did it take to walk through that door into the mission field? What is it taking to stay there? Her companion picked her up the first afternoon at the mission home. They drove deeper and deeper into the inner city. Gang markings blocked out territory. From time to time they witnessed furtive drug sales. More than once when they would return home at night, flashing lights and sirens would announce that someone else on her block had been beaten. She found sadness, poverty, desperation, and despair. The air hung thick in darkness. *What am I doing here?* she wondered.

Her first week she was welcomed by amoebic dysentery. No one invited her to stay in bed and get well. She gobbled pills and worked fourteen hours a day with a hungry piranha chomping in her guts. Spiders infested her closets, her clothing, her sheets. The first month, the city sewage backed up and filled the bathtub in her apartment. A month later the pipes broke and flooded the floors. One evening a member flicked a cockroach out of her long blonde hair, and she wrote that she had become so accustomed to the bugs that she didn't even flinch.

How does she stay? She confesses that she thinks daily about coming home. "There is only one reason I can do this," she wrote. "It is *not* because of social pressure. It certainly is not because it is easy or because I like it." (Of course, she has grown to love the members and investigators whose lives have intertwined with hers. But that alone would not be enough.) "It is only because I love the Lord, and I know this is where I am supposed to be."

The Wrestling Champion of Niue Island

DEAN L. THOMSON

*𝒯*he island of Niue Fekai is in the South Pacific near the center of Polynesia. At the time I served a mission there, it was headquarters of the Niue Island District of the Tongan Mission, and The Church of Jesus Christ of Latter-day Saints had been on the island less than six years. . . .

One memorable day my missionary companion and I were returning from the back of the island when we chanced upon a large crowd on the . . . green near the center of the village of Alofi. From the perimeter of the crowd, I could see six big barefooted natives dressed in khaki shorts, preparing for a wrestling contest.

Suddenly I heard my name called. The pastor of the island's London Missionary Church was pointing at me over the heads of the crowd and beckoning me to enter the circle. It was then that a horrible suspicion entered my mind. The pastor explained to the natives in their own tongue (which by this time I was understanding only too well) that since the Caucasians had not been represented in their contest, it was fitting that Eleta Tomosoni (Elder Thomson) should do the honors. Looking at those six men from within the circle, I thought I had stumbled onto a South Pacific branch of the Los Angeles Rams. When I heard the rules being read for the finals in the Niue Island Wrestling Championship, I thought I was finished! What was even more disconcerting was the fact that I had been teaching the boys in our branches of the Church to wrestle so they could compete as sportsmen, with good sportsmanship being stressed. In the crowd I saw some of the faces of those boys who had been in my wrestling sessions. Like a skunk turning upwind, I realized that I could not back out gracefully.

I finally agreed to wrestle one of the men—but was further disheartened to learn I would have to wrestle all six! Names were being drawn out of a hat to determine in which order they were to be wrestled, not just which one would compete.

At that moment the full force of their size emerged. With my six-foot, 200-pound frame I had ranked in the upper percentile of the male population of the world, but now I observed that I was the same size as the smallest of the six Niuean village champions.

I glanced toward my companion. He was about 150 pounds and five-foot-seven or so. No support from that quarter. Placing my hands beneath my chin in a prayer-like fashion, I indicated to him that we needed all the help we could get. He responded by looking at his watch—I suppose to see how long it would take for the wrestlers to annihilate me.

I drew the first name, which belonged to one of the largest of my opponents. He stepped out of the group and squared off, as I quickly rehearsed the rules in my mind. Somehow I had to get him down with both of his shoulder blades touching the ground—that was all. I did not even have to hold him down while someone counted to three in Niuean or English.

The handkerchief was dropped, and he was running at me. From that point the facts slip into oblivion. I recalled his coming at me, and I vaguely remember getting hold of him and using his own momentum to throw him off balance and to the ground. Afterward, try as I will, I cannot recall anything else that happened until well after the contest was over. Later my companion told me that he had been watching his watch, and when the referee dropped his handkerchief, the time started; when the opponent was downed, the clock was stopped. It had taken a cumulative total of 47 seconds for me to down that entire battery of native warriors, and I was the Niue Island Wrestling Champion!

There is no question in my mind what happened. Before the contest, we had been harassed, rocks had been thrown at us, and we had been chased out of native villages with bush knives. But now there was a perceptible change. The natives would go out of their way to greet us with the Niuean *fakaalofa,* or greeting. We were on the way to being accepted. Through the Spirit of the Lord, one missionary had been rescued, and the way had been opened for missionary work on Niue Island.

The Fruits of Faith

KARL R. KOERNER

$\mathscr{B}$renda Lin was only a high school graduate when she left the city of Chia-Yi in central Taiwan to work in the Taipei Grand Hyatt Hotel. She felt intimidated working in the hotel's executive business offices where most of the people around her had more education and spoke better English than she did. She decided to attend a free English class—one taught by foreign missionaries at the Mormon Church. It wasn't long before she made a few changes in her life, listened to the discussions, and joined the Church.

From the beginning, Brenda was very missionary-minded. As she worked from day to day, she often wondered if she should serve a mission. It was a tough decision because her parents were dead set against her going. When she shared with them the idea of this altruistic adventure, she was met with an extremely negative, but not surprising, reaction. Her parent's beliefs followed the traditional Chinese practice of worshipping ancestors and idols. Christianity was merely something they had been superficially exposed to during their lives.

Still, Brenda kept working and praying about her desire to serve a mission.

Shortly afterwards, she had an interesting experience when an ill-fitting contact lens caused her a great deal of pain in one eye. As she thought about her own physical pain, she realized that her parents would experience emotional pain if they were separated from her while she served a mission. She also realized that many of the challenges that come with missionary service would also cause emotional pain for parents who are unfamiliar with the Church.

She felt greater empathy for her parents and continued to pray about the mission. Finally, she received the answer that a mission was definitely what the Lord wanted her to do and that, with time, the hearts of her parents would be softened. She decided to broach the subject with them one more time, hoping they could start to understand how wonderful and worthwhile this missionary experience would be. Unfortunately, it didn't work. Her mother even said: "If you will only forget about the mission, you can have anything you want. We will help you go to graduate school, you can travel wherever you desire, you don't have to work, and we will give you all the money you need."

Even though she knew she was going against her parent's wishes, Brenda still felt strongly that she was doing what the Lord wanted her to do. She soon received her mission call to the Taiwan Taichung Mission in the southern half of Taiwan—the same area where her parents lived.

She shared her history with the mission president. By

this time, her parents had disowned her and wouldn't have anything to do with her. It was hard to be a missionary under these circumstances because she loved her parents so much. Her heart ached as she thought about the rift between them. Other missionaries received supportive letters and encouragement, even occasional packages. She didn't receive anything from home; her parents would not answer her letters. The mission president gave her special permission to call home once a month. But when she tried to call her parents, they would hang up. Brenda found solace in her associations with friends from church and her devotion to her Heavenly Father.

Several months went by. She lost herself in missionary work and was blessed with great success. Finally, nearly a year after starting her mission and after countless unanswered letters and phone calls, things began to change. Her parents warmed up and let the local bishop visit them. They invited some of the missionaries over for dinner. Brenda's prayers for them were indeed being answered.

A few months later, Brenda asked if she could make a special call home. Her father had been diagnosed with a rare intestinal disorder and needed surgery right away. Doctors said there was a 90 percent chance he would not survive the operation. The whole mission prayed for her father. Through his daughter, he was taught about the nature of our Father in Heaven and of faith; though not a member, he was given a priesthood blessing by the local elders. Miraculously, he had a full recovery.

Eighteen months soon came to an end, and it was

time for Brenda to be released. One of the most memorable occasions for the mission president and his wife was when Brenda's parents came to the mission home to pick her up. In the living room of the mission home, the president told her parents what a great missionary their daughter had been and how she had helped so many people. The pride in their eyes at their daughter's accomplishments was obvious. It had been a spiritual experience for them too. They had learned so much, and grown so much—even though they were far from becoming members, the respect was there. It was a good start.

Later, as Brenda Lin sat in the San Diego Temple waiting to be sealed to Jacob for time and eternity, she thought back to all that had happened. She was so grateful for the gospel. The future would not be without problems, but she had learned how to approach and resolve them.

"Why Do You Want to Go on This Mission, Son?"

HAROLD B. LEE

*W*hile I was attending a stake conference, I was to interview some of the prospective missionaries. Before one boy came to see me, the stake president said, "Now here is a boy who has just come through a serious experience. He is just out of the service. He suffered shell-shock in battle, and I think we need to talk pretty carefully to him and make certain that he is prepared to go."

So as I talked with the young man, I said, "Why do you want to go on this mission, son? Are you sure that you really want to go, after all the harrowing experiences you have had?"

He sat thoughtfully for a few moments and then said, "Brother Lee, I had never been away from home when I went into the service, and when I got out into the camps, every waking hour I heard filthy, profane language. I found myself losing a certain pure-mindedness, and I sought God in prayer to give me the strength not to fall into that terrible habit. God heard my prayer and gave me strength. Then we went through basic training, and I asked Him to give me physical strength to continue, and He did. He heard my prayer. As we moved up toward the fighting lines and I could hear the booming of the guns and the crackling of the rifles, I was afraid. Again I prayed to God to give me the courage to do the task that I was there to do, and He heard my prayer and gave me courage.

"When I was sent up with an advance patrol to search out the enemies and to send back for the reinforcements, telling them where to attack—and sometimes the enemy would almost hedge me around until I was cut off, and it seemed that there was no escape—I thought that surely my life would be taken. I asked for the only force of power to guide me safely back, and God heard me. Time and again through the most harrowing experiences He led me back. Now," he said, "I am back home. I have recovered, and I would like to give thanks to that power to which I prayed—God, our Heavenly Father. Going out on a mission, I can teach others that faith which I was taught in Sunday School, in seminary, in my priesthood class, and in my home. I want to teach others so that they will have that same strength that guided me through this difficult experience."

The Courage of a Martyr

BRYANT S. HINCKLEY

Editor's Note: The following account was related to Bryant S. Hinckley by President Rudger Clawson, who served with Elder Joseph Standing in the Southern States Mission for only a short time before they were instructed to go to Rome, Georgia, for a district conference. The incident that follows occurred during travels associated with that conference.

$\mathcal{T}$he morning of July 21, 1879, dawned bright and beautiful. It was Sunday—peace permeated the very atmosphere they breathed. There was a calmness and a spirit of tranquillity that was in keeping with the Holy day; it was, however, but the calm that precedes the cyclone.

. . . The young missionaries started on their journey. Peace was in their youthful hearts. They carried the message of good will toward all men. They were young, alone, unarmed, and far from home. Their only armor of defense was the truth. As they walked through the primeval woods of Georgia with the feeling that all the trouble was over, they made a turn in the road and suddenly came in view of an armed mob.

With shouts and vile imprecations the mob charged down upon them. The leader said: "You are our prisoners." Elder Standing replied: "By what authority do you arrest us upon the public highway? If you have a warrant for our arrest we should like to see it." The answer was: "The United States of America is 'agin' you and there is no law in Georgia for the Mormons. You go with us." "We'll show you by what authority we act!" some of them shouted.

The mobocrats led the way and the missionaries followed. Elder Standing was greatly agitated. He was deathly pale and moved nervously and quickly all the time, endeavoring to explain to the mob the nature of their mission, what they were doing—expostulating with them to no avail. Elder Clawson walked more deliberately and slowly, which seemed to exasperate one of the fiends behind him who gave him a heavy blow on the back of the head which almost felled him to the ground. A few minutes later this same murderer raised a heavy club and was about to deliver a death-dealing blow to this innocent man when one of the mob caught his arm. This vicious fellow had already flourished a cocked pistol menacingly in Elder Clawson's face accompanied with oaths and threats. . . .

We quote the words of President Clawson:

"The fateful moment had arrived. The three men on horses rode up. The presumption is that they had left the party shortly after our arrest for the purpose of locating a secluded place in the forest to carry out the intent of the mob. . . . The spokesman with a rifle in his trembling hands, for he appeared greatly agitated, said:

'Follow us.' . . . At that critical instant, Joseph Standing jumped to his feet, turned and faced the horsemen, clasped his hands firmly together, and said in a commanding voice, 'Surrender.'

"As the word 'Surrender' left the lips of Joseph Standing, one of the men sitting in the circle pointed his weapon at Elder Standing and fired. Elder Standing, whirling in his tracks, fell heavily to the ground face downward, and immediately turned upon his back with his face upward. The mobocrats instantly stood upon their feet. A cloud of smoke and dust enveloped the body of the wounded man. At this critical juncture the leading mobocrat, pointing at me, said: 'Shoot that man.' Every weapon was leveled at my head. My time had come, so it seemed to me. My turn to follow Joseph Standing was at hand. The command to shoot had been given. I was looking down the gun barrels of the murderous mobs. I folded my arms and said: 'Shoot,' and almost persuaded myself that I was shot, so intense were my feelings.

"I quickly recovered my presence of mind when I heard the voice of a mobocrat which said hurriedly and in a tone of fear: 'Don't shoot.'

"I then stepped over to the spot where Joseph Standing had fallen. . . . I saw at a glance that he was beyond all earthly help. . . . "

Suddenly the mob appeared to sense the horrible character of the deed they had committed, and seized with consternation they instinctively rushed together in a compact group as if seeking mutual protection. Elder Clawson walked over to where Elder Standing was lying, stooped and looked into his face. He was breathing heavily. He raised the dying man's head, and tenderly placed his hat under it to keep it out of the dust. An awful sense of grief and utter loneliness seized him; he could only put his trust in God. He exclaimed: "Gentlemen, it is a burning shame to leave a man to die in these woods this way. For Heaven's sake, either you go and secure assistance that the body may be removed and cared for or allow me to do so." After a moment's consultation they said: "You go."

Elder Clawson set out at once to find the coroner. It took him from ten o'clock in the morning until sunset to get the coroner and his assistants to the place where the body lay. He says: "I was horrified to discover that the mob had returned—presumably while Elder Standing was yet alive—and had fired several shots into his face and neck." The coroner's jury, after due deliberation, rendered a verdict to the effect that Joseph Standing met his death from gun shots fired by a mob—giving their names. The body was then released. . . .

The coroner before leaving said: "Mr. Clawson, why don't you bury the body here in Georgia? After some years you can take up the bones and move them to Utah." He said, "Never, never, never! I am going to do for my companion what he would do for me under like circumstances. I tell you frankly, Mr. Coroner, if I had been shot to death in Georgia, as he was shot to death, I would not wish to be buried in this soil. I am sure Joseph Standing feels that way. I am going to take his body home." . . .

Quoting from Brother Clawson:

"It became my duty to prepare the body. I had never before touched a dead person, and yet there was no help for it. Under the feeble light of several candles I washed the body. With painstaking care I washed the wounds. To me it was a painful ordeal—but willingly and tenderly performed."

It was far into the dark before he completed this sad and difficult service. This was a supreme test of his loyalty to his companion. All who read this story must know that Rudger Clawson in a supreme and crucial hour displayed the spirit and courage of a martyr.

The Men Were Masked

JOHN ALEXANDER

*O*n the morning of the first of June, I left
Brother Reed's about three miles from Adairsville,
Georgia. . . . I told him I would like to go to Adairsville
and see if I could make an appointment to preach, as we
had never held any meetings in that neighborhood. I
talked to a few farmers along the road, but the results
were not satisfactory, and when about a mile from
Adairsville I started to return to Brother Reed's.

About halfway between the two places, as I was
singing aloud one of our hymns, I was startled by a
noise and saw three masked men step out of a thicket
and face me (the road here passed through a forest).
This was about eleven o'clock in the morning. The men
were masked by having what appeared to be some
unbleached calico tied around their faces, under their
eyes, and which hung down to their breasts. Their hats
were pulled down over their foreheads to conceal the
upper portions of their faces. One of the men was a slim
man, over six feet high, I believe, who seemed the leader;

the other two men were men about five feet nine or ten inches.

When about ten feet from me, the tallest man said, "Are you one of those Mormon elders from Utah?" I told him I was. He replied, "You go up there in the brush."

I answered, "I don't feel like going up. What do you want me to go for?"

At this he blurted out, "You go. I won't tell you again."

He then drew his pistol and covered me. The other two followed his example. I walked into the brush fifty yards the way they pointed. Then I stopped and turned around. The leader told me to go on. I told him I had gone as far as I was going. At this they drew their pistols and presented them at my face, about four feet off. . . . I . . . said, "For God's sake, men, you don't mean to kill a young, innocent man. What have I done?"

The leader answered, "Well, you, you came out here preaching false doctrine, and you know it's false, and say that it is."

I replied, "No, sir, I don't think it's false; I know it is not false, and I can't say that it is."

He said, "Well, you're going to die right here; have you anything to say?" I told him if they meant to kill me, I had something to say. He continued, "Well, what is it?"

I asked him, "Will you allow me to offer up a few words of prayer?"

"Yes," he said, "if you'll be quick about it."

I . . . said, "Oh, my God, if it is thy will that these men should take my life, I am willing to die," and a few more words that I do not recollect. I then . . . looked them straight in the face.

As they lowered their pistols, one pointing to my face, another lower, I closed my eyes. The moment my eyes closed, three shots were fired. I recollect hearing the reports, but nothing after. My senses seemed taken away. I felt myself falling but do not recollect striking the ground.

When I came to, the first thing I remember was that I was on my hands and knees looking around. I arose to my feet. I ran, or rather staggered or stumbled, down to the road. I did not know which way I was going or where I was going, but I kept on until I found myself at Brother Reed's fence; that was the first time I realized where I was. I there fell exhausted, and Brother Reed came, picked me up, and carried me into the house. . . . Brother Reed and his family took the greatest care of me. . . .

Of the three shots, one went through the front of my hat (a low-crowned, black and white straw). As I was a little up the hill and the hat was slightly tilted back, the ball went in at the front and almost immediately came out of the crown, giving the appearance of glancing upwards. This was the shot fired by the leader, who I noticed had his pistol pointed at my head. My coat was rather open, and the second bullet passed through it on the left side, just grazing the slide of my watch chain. The third ball did not touch me.

When the three men shot, they were standing in a row about twelve steps from me.

Returning Home

CARLFRED BRODERICK

$\mathcal{I}$ was in a foreign country giving a workshop for others in my profession [counseling]. The workshop was over, and I was just exhausted. . . . The telephone rang. It was the mission president, who also was a general authority whom I had never met, but who had read in the paper that I was there. He had a problem with one of his sister missionaries. Although he'd been working with her, she had a ticket to go home on the same flight I was on. He'd labored with her and given her blessings. She'd only been out six weeks, but she was going home and nothing he was able to say changed her mind. The mission president said, "She said she had your text in college, and I told her you were here. I asked her if she would see you, and she said she would." . . . He said to me, "We'll send the car for you."

This sister and I sat down together. She had her purse clutched and her ticket prominently displayed on it. She looked at me a bit defiantly, and I said, "The president tells me you're headed for home."

She answered, "Yes, and you can't talk me out of it either."

I said, "Why?"

She told me why.

It was an awful story. She did grow up in a Mormon family in Idaho—a farm family, a rural, poor family. She had been sexually abused, not just by her father, but by all her male relatives. She was terribly abused. . . .

Finally, when she was fourteen . . . the bishop took her out of that home into his own home where she finished her high school years; he sent her to college, and then she went on a mission. Her father's "patriarchal blessing" when she left his home was this, "Well, aren't we fine folk now? Gonna go live with the bishop and all those holy joes over on the other side of town. Well, let me just tell you something, girl, and don't you never forget it. They can't make a silk purse out of a sow's ear." That's what she decided on her mission. She decided she didn't belong there with all those silk purses. . . . She was having feelings that she believed were unworthy and told herself, "My daddy was right. You can take a girl out of a family and send her to college, you can send her on a mission, but you can't change what she is—a sow's ear."

So she was going home to throw herself away because she didn't belong out here pretending to be someone she wasn't. I said to her, "Before you came on your mission, you went to the temple, didn't you? You were anointed to become a queen, weren't you, a princess in your Heavenly Father's house? That's no way to treat a princess. There may be—I can't imagine it—but there may be some justification in their backgrounds for the way those men treated you when you were young. I don't know; I can't imagine any. But, I'm confident of this, the Lord will not easily forgive you if you treat His daughter that way. You're going to throw her away, a princess of our Heavenly Father? Then what are you going to say to Him when He says, 'How have you handled the stewardship that I gave you of this glorious personage who lived with me, who is my daughter, who is a royal personage of dignity and of honor? I sent her down to the earth, and how have you brought her back to me?'" She with the eloquence of her age and circumstances started to cry, but she stayed.

I saw her in Provo two or three years later when I was there speaking. She asked if I remembered her, and I did . . . and said, "How are you doing?" She answered, "I'm growing just as fast as I can. I thought you'd want to know." She understood who she was. I told her that I felt her stewardship was to get that daughter of our Heavenly Father home, home to Heavenly Father, home where she belonged.

"What If the Church Isn't True?"

ROBERT L. MILLET

*W*hile serving as a missionary in the Eastern States, my senior companion and I entered a town in New Jersey and began a systematic program of door-to-door contacting. We had not worked in the area for many days before it became obvious that the local Protestant ministers had prepared their parishioners for our coming. At almost every door we would be greeted with, "Oh, you must be the Mormons. Here, we have something for you." They would then hand us an anti-Mormon tract. We collected literally hundreds of these pamphlets and stacked them in the corner of our apartment. Curiosity eventually got the best of us, and both of us decided to peruse some of the material. There were many things we read that were disturbing, but I remember most of all an issue regarding the LDS view of the Godhead that caused me extreme uneasiness. My companion was no less disturbed than I. Day after day we went about our task of knocking on doors, being rejected and rebuffed, and expanding our collection of anti-Mormon propaganda. When I had reached the point of spiritual discomfort where I couldn't stand the tension any longer, I said to my companion at lunch: "Elder Henderson, what if the Church isn't true?" I expected him to be startled by such a question. He was not. He responded: "I've been wondering the same thing." Now I *was* startled. He was my senior companion, my leader, my example. "What if the Baptist Church is right?" I asked. "What if the Catholics have had priesthood authority all along?" "I don't know what to say," he replied. It was a depressing time for both of us.

I can still remember how very intense and focused my prayers were during those difficult days. I pleaded with God to give me an answer, to give me a feeling, to give me something! I lifted my voice heavenward constantly—on my knees whenever I had occasion and in my heart all through the day. For over two weeks we struggled. I had concluded—though I had not expressed this to my companion—that unless some resolution to my soul-searching came soon, I would go home. I felt then that I just couldn't be a hypocrite, that I couldn't bear testimony of something I didn't know was true. . . . The questions I had in regard to the Godhead were eating me alive. I was confused, ashamed, and terribly uncomfortable. One afternoon as we came home for lunch I sat in the easy chair in the small living room in the apartment. I propped my feet up, sat back, let out a sigh, and for some reason picked up a copy of the pamphlet, "Joseph Smith Tells His Own Story." I opened the brochure and began reading. I was not five lines into the

Prophet's opening statement before I was absolutely wrapped in a feeling of warmth and comfort that I had never known, almost as though someone had covered me with a type of spiritual blanket. Though I heard no words, the feelings that came to me seemed to voice the following: "Of course this work is true. You know it is true. And now, as to your question, be patient. You'll understand soon enough." This was all I needed for the time being. It was inspiration. It was perspective. I shared my newfound faith with Elder Henderson, he felt a similar spirit of comfort, and we went about our task with more courage in our conviction. The difficult matter had been put on a shelf. The answer to my question, by the way, did come in time. Within a year I was blessed with a companion who thoroughly understood the issue and helped me to see an aspect of the gospel that to me had previously been a mystery.

Songs from the Heart

NAME WITHHELD

$\mathscr{A}$aron is the fourth child in a family of six children. He is totally deaf in one ear and impaired in the other. Over the years, his "good" ear has gradually worsened, bringing him dangerously close to profound deafness in both ears.

Those who are deaf know that there is no easy way to make distinctions among various levels of hearing loss. In deaf culture, people are quick to ask, "Are you deaf or hearing-impaired?" For them, being deaf is not a matter of the documented hearing loss shown on an audiogram. Instead, you are classified as deaf if you use sign language rather than speech, regardless of how much you really can hear. The big distinction between *deaf* and *hearing-impaired* is whether you use a regular telephone. Those who are deaf classify Aaron as hearing-impaired because he speaks, reads lips, and uses the phone. He discovered on his mission, however, that his hearing was actually worse than most of the deaf people he worked with and taught.

During the first months of his mission, although he

taught and baptized people, his companionships were rough. In the past, he had survived by working hard and tenaciously following rules with exactness. He had a strong testimony. His lack of social finesse was evident as he expressed himself, and he often said exactly what he thought. Companions who did not want to keep the rules or do the work thought these traits made Aaron hard to get along with. These problems were compounded by his hearing loss. Companions complained about how hard it was to work with Aaron because he often interrupted conversations, he talked too much, he changed the subject all the time, and he didn't fit in.

We acknowledged to the mission president that Aaron did have some flaws, as do our other five children. Like many families, we had learned to work around each other's faults quite successfully and had made accommodations for the special circumstances related to his deafness. We explained that Aaron interrupted conversations because he was not always aware that someone was talking. He changes the subject sometimes because he thinks someone has said "Thursday" when they have actually said "thirsty." He talks a lot because that way he knows what is being said. But, we pointed out, he also has a testimony. He had read the Book of Mormon. He had gone on a mission because he loves the Lord and wanted to serve. He had kept his body pure. And he would be willing to work until he dropped. Surely those qualified him to be a missionary, even if it was sometimes necessary to compensate for his handicap.

In the end, even with our efforts to provide a greater understanding of the causes of Aaron's behavior and with suggestions of practical ways to work through the challenges of his deafness, we were told that no one was willing to work with him.

It was a surprise when three weeks later we heard our son's voice on our answering machine. "I'm at the airport . . . on my way to another mission . . . I'll write you about it when I find out what is happening." Aaron arrived in his new area, not knowing anything except that he had been sent away. Months later, his loving mission president explained that this transfer was an answer to prayer. The mission president had prayed for the ability to serve the needs of the members of the deaf community in his area. Then Aaron came to the mission and, not long after, another elder, profoundly deaf from birth, was transferred there to finish the last six months of his mission. Together, these fine elders labored with and loved the deaf saints in their new area.

The last fourteen months of Aaron's mission were productive and happy. My husband and I decided to pick him up from his mission. What a blessing it was to be with him on his last day. I had never seen him sign until he bore his testimony in his final transfer meeting. He looked so different. Through all the mission ups and downs he had matured and softened. There was a sweet peacefulness in his demeanor that had not been there two years earlier. His strong testimony had blossomed further. He had developed a valuable second language, American Sign Language, which will continue to bless him and others.

At home a few weeks later, we inquired about the difficulties of his mission. He said that he knew there were bad experiences but he could not remember them very well. Pressing him further, he said "It all seems normal to me. That's my life."

At his homecoming sacrament meeting, he spoke of an important lesson he had learned as a missionary. He told about the labeling that goes on in the deaf culture to differentiate those who are deaf from those who are hearing or hearing-impaired. He concluded that he did not fit in any of these categories. Instead, he was a child of our Heavenly Father and that gave him great peace and comfort.

As our daughter played the piano at Aaron's homecoming and our four other sons began to sing, Aaron sang along, using his beautiful, sensitive sign language. The congregation was touched as he sang silently with his hands. And we knew that Aaron had finally found a way to express the songs of his heart.

The Spirit Is Willing

Joy for the "Chemo" Queen

JOANNE BAIR

$\mathscr{I}$ am a five and one-half year ovarian cancer survivor and I celebrate life, its goodness, its beauty.

During a complete hysterectomy, my doctors found a tumor so entangled in my internal organs that it burst while being removed. I went through chemotherapy five days each month for four months. I had almost no side effects—no sickness or hair loss. Six months later, the cancer was back. A CAT scan revealed two golf-ball-sized tumors. A six-month course of chemotherapy was advised, which meant two days each month in the hospital. When I first went to the hospital to begin this second chemo cycle, I was hit by a jolt of reality. As I was checking in, I saw the words *ovarian cancer* on my chart. There it was—official. Right then I made a commitment to survive. I thought, "I'll deal with this, and with the help of the Lord, I'll make it."

This second chemo experience was not at all like the first. I had nearly every side effect possible—deathly nausea, blinding headaches, chills, fever, shortness of breath, mouth sores, loss of hearing, constipation, neuropathy, and hair loss. Every bone in my body ached and screamed. I wondered how I could endure six months, especially since I also have arthritis, osteoporosis, and scoliosis. Alma's words helped: "I do know that whosoever shall put their trust in God shall be supported in their trials, and their troubles, and their afflictions, and shall be lifted up at the last day" (Alma 36:3). I survived those thirty treatments. A CAT scan revealed no tumors. Here was joy again, joy and thanksgiving.

Eight months later, the cancer was back. Another CAT scan revealed spots on the liver and liquid in the pleural area of the lungs. Where was joy now?

For days I pictured different scenarios from the future, and I was not in any of them. But my faith remained deep and strong. I prayed to Father in Heaven for strength, for insight into my situation, for the doctors to make meaningful decisions. At this point "things" weren't important anymore, staying alive was. I felt I just wasn't ready to leave this world yet. I wanted to fight. Yes, I could do it. I would do it. Joy returned! I repeated often the phrase "Cancer is NOT a death sentence."

More chemo? Why not? I couldn't quit. There was so much hope. So many chemicals yet to try. I started this third cycle of chemo almost four years ago and continue presently. Perhaps I'll set a world record of surviving the most chemo treatments ever. I've had 230 individual treatments in this third cycle, and 230 days of coming through the clouds of chemo into the sunlight of feeling good again. It's become a way of life.

The chemo is not my only weapon, however. I also

use my faith and my mind as antigens. I believe that God wants us to have healthy strong bodies and that if we do all in our power to learn and to help ourselves, he will succor us and comfort us. A positive attitude and our strong faith make us receptive to the healing influence. Hope is an essential part of the will to live. Of course negative thoughts do occur occasionally. Would I be normal if they didn't? But I know that uncertainty and doubt depress the immune system, and I can't let that happen! I do find it helpful if I talk about my cancer. I think it helps to vocalize feelings and I'm happy my friends are interested enough to ask.

I know I'm buying time with the positive approach, and that's important, but being positive won't cure cancer. It can, however, change the way I live my life and the way I feel about my cancer. Cancer can't negatively change who we are unless we let it. With or without cancer, each of us must use what we have at this particular moment in time to live life to its fullest. It is not what we have in life but what we do with what we have that counts.

There is joy in knowing that I have received answers from the Lord to my pleas for strength and guidance in this continuing challenge. I have felt joy in recovery, joy in enduring, joy in discovery. If my time here is cut short, I will put aside the torments of my body for a step into real joy—eternal life.

The "University of Disability"

MARILYNNE LINFORD

*W*hen Margaret Van Noy was born the doctor and nurses whisked her away so that her mother wouldn't see her. Her mother was moved to a single-occupant room—unusual in 1950—and when she asked to see her baby, the doctor told her that the baby, a girl, would soon die because of severe physical complications. Doctors told the new mother that her daughter was mentally retarded as well. Nonetheless, the parents named their new little girl Margaret—after her mother—and somewhere during the weeks and months that followed, Margaret's bright and happy intellect emerged, bringing tremendous delight to her parents and defying the doctor's predictions.

Margaret is now three feet, seven inches tall because she has very short legs. Her right arm ends just above the elbow. Her left arm is shorter than you'd expect. She has two fingers and a thumb on her left hand. She has had twenty-eight or so operations. She lost count.

When she was twenty-one she went to her bishop and

told him that she wanted to go on a mission. Her bishop talked to the stake president. The papers were soon processed and after waiting and waiting—the call took a month to come—she received a call to Dallas, Texas. When she showed the call to her father, he became very upset. He didn't want her to face additional problems or rejection. He made her promise to do nothing but work in the office.

At the Mission Home in Salt Lake (in the days before the MTC), the mission president's wife told her that she shouldn't be on a mission. She told her she wasn't suited for it physically or emotionally. As she left the Mission Home the president said, "Do not proselyte in the public sector." But Margaret was determined. She arrived in Dallas, and was welcomed by her new mission president.

Margaret said that meeting her first companion made her feel like she was at home. But missionary work wasn't what she expected. All she and her companion did all day was visit members. She said, "It wasn't until I got my second companion that I learned that [the mission president] had told both companions not to tract with me. But I wanted to tract. I wanted to bear my testimony to everyone not just members." When Margaret finally learned this, her new response was, "Forget that. We're tracting." And so they did.

"We had some wonderful experiences," Margaret remembers. "I expected rejection but because of my condition, we got in lots of doors.

"When my eighteen months were up, I had an exit interview with [my president]. He asked me what my future plans were. I told him that I wanted to go home and get married. (I figured that the boys would have matured and one of them would be able to see me for who I was and not just my disabilities.) He said, 'You will never marry in this life.' I started to cry and cry. When I got back to BYU all I could see were couples, couples, couples—couples here, couples there, couples everywhere. It was very hard. I fell into a deep depression. I refused to go to any activities, just to class and home. One day a voice spoke to me and said, 'Margaret, why do you want to get married.' I answered 'because I want to be happy.' The voice said, 'You don't have to be married to be happy. Happiness is something that comes from within.' I recognized the voice of the Holy Ghost and was so grateful; a huge burden had been lifted, and it's never bothered me since."

She worked hard and graduated from BYU and got a job using her Latin, doing genealogy research for the church for six years. Someone suggested to her that she get a job at Deseret Industries. Her first thoughts were, "Heck no. D.I. is a place for handicapped people. But I got desperate and I applied. They hired me in dispatch, supervising all the drivers on the dock. I enjoyed my work and stayed at that job for thirteen years, then they promoted me to my current position."

When she was thirty, her father called and said, "How would you like to learn to drive?" He invented a way to bring the brake and gas pedals up with rods and taught her to drive. She could hardly see over the dashboard and dented the car on every side. But she learned. At present, she drives back and forth to work each day.

"I've learned to look at people as I think the Lord looks at them," she says. "I see them completely differently than I would if I hadn't been schooled in the University of Disability myself. Nothing shocks me anymore. I don't look at people and say or even think, 'This is your fault.' I don't blame. I don't make judgments. I just try to help. I know to others I am disabled, but I don't feel that way. This is who I am. I don't know why I was born with this body. I think that I made the decision in the premortal life to have this body for my earth-existence perhaps to guarantee that I return to Heavenly Father. I call it 'my vehicle to the Celestial Kingdom.'

"I still have a long way to go. I still have much to overcome. But I like who I am and have discovered that there is something sweet about struggling through life and feeling the Holy Ghost all the time. His support is constant. I feel whole. My needs are taken care of. I am really blessed."

"Please Don't Let Me Be Paralyzed"

DONNA BOSS LINFORD

It was my fifty-seventh wedding anniversary, 1 June 1995, and just two weeks after I'd been to my doctor and received a clean bill of health. I recall him saying, "Donna, most people would die for your blood pressure and cholesterol numbers." I had been in very good health all my life. My great joy of the past year had been attending classes at the University of Utah. Today was the last day of my third quarter. At this specific moment in time I was ready to leave the condo to go to the copy shop to make a copy of a final paper when I noticed that my left shoe was untied. I bent down to tie it.

Suddenly something was wrong. I couldn't make my left arm move. A panicky, sick, frightening feeling filled me. I felt cold and started to shake violently. I knew I was having a stroke. I had no headache, no dizziness, no pain anywhere, but my heart was beating so hard and so fast I thought I was going to die right then. I prayed

"Father in Heaven, please, please don't let me become paralyzed."

I called my daughter-in-law. "I'm so scared," were the first words out of my mouth. After quickly assessing what was wrong, she said, "Hang up and I'll call the paramedics." I thought that while I was still conscious I should open the door for them. I crawled to the door and recall the sensation of needles pricking me all over. I remember seeing strangers coming towards me, but those are my last memories for several weeks. When recognition began to come to me I was shocked to realize that I couldn't move my left side at all. I *was* paralyzed. My worst fear had become reality. I had constant, terrible nightmares and spent most of my time praying for strength to get through each long day and each longer night.

Every morning someone would take me from my hospital bed to therapy. I asked if I'd ever walk again and the answer was no. Days lengthened into weeks, weeks into months. Time crawled. I prayed every hour of every day to be able to become whole again. My son and my husband gave me a number of priesthood blessings. Still, loneliness and fear engulfed me constantly. The only relief came when I prayed. I pled with the Lord to make my arm, my leg, and my swallowing normal again. Besides everything else I was dealing with, I'd lost the ability to swallow.

My thoughts also went to my mother who had told me many times before her death that we all must go through a refining fire to cleanse us from pride and make us worthy to meet our Maker. Now I faced the truth. I did have too much pride and I placed too much importance on material things. I knew I needed to read and study the scriptures more. I knew I needed to think much more of others and give more service to mankind. I found myself begging God to forgive me and give me another chance. My husband, Bill, brought scriptures and read to me every night before he left, which brought peace. Slowly, so slowly, I mean so very slowly, I started to get a bit of strength and could see a very small amount of progress. I was the kind who always needed everything done yesterday. The stroke was teaching me patience as part of my personal purging process.

Five wedding and stroke anniversaries have come and gone. With very hard work and God's help, I relearned to write. I can now stand up by my wheelchair; I can climb stairs with Bill holding on to my safety belt; I can walk down eighteen steps with my cane. Bill bought me a computer, and with my right hand I can work the mouse and write e-mails to my children and grand-children. My mind is clear and active, and I am enjoying life more than I can tell you. The stroke was the best thing that has ever happened to me. I appreciate the refining education it has been. I read, listen to great music, and write poetry.

The stroke has given me the opportunity to develop my poetry talent, which I really did not know was there, and learn to use a computer at age eighty-one. My family is helping me make a book of my poetry.

The stroke has taught me patience, empathy, and understanding. I thank my Father in Heaven that I've been able to adjust to a completely new way of life.

I have a strong testimony of the gospel of Jesus Christ. I know it is the only solid foundation left on this earth. I know that one day I will be made whole and be completely restored to good health if I prove worthy. I am grateful my life was spared and try daily to keep the promises I made to my Father in Heaven while I was in the hospital.

Alive and Still Kicking

KATHY ENSIGN ENGLAND

*T*hree years ago, my parents hosted an "I'm alive and still kicking!" party in my honor. Five years before then, I'd been told to write my will and plan on the grave. Angiograms of my brain suggested that I had contracted Eastern Equine Viral Encephalitis from a mosquito bite on a trip to Florida. I'd gone into a coma-like condition, and the doctors predicted three possibilities, *if* I ever woke up: severe mental impairment, severe physical impairment, or both.

When I finally awoke, unable even to roll over or sit up—but still able to think and talk, to laugh and cry—I discovered that the encephalitis virus had damaged most of my motor movement and coordination nerves. I was stuck in a wheelchair. My speech was slurred. One of the specialists said that only 5 percent of the people with my kind of encephalitis made it past the five-year mark. So that was the reason for our celebration! I'm now on my eighth year and counting!

I'm still in a wheelchair. My husband of twenty years divorced me. My three sons live with him. Besides the nerve paralysis, I've also had sugar diabetes since I was a child. Life has not been easy.

Initially, I found myself praying to die. Fast, quick, clean. It just seemed easier. But then, I realized how stubborn I was being, and told the Lord I would accept whatever his will and his timing were . . . (only *please* help me to get well fast!) I began bargaining with the Lord. If you do . . . , I'll do. . . . Nothing big or dramatic happened. Why wasn't he healing me?

Desperate, I continued praying hard, trying to figure out what else *I* could do. I had never been able to fast before because of my diabetes, but I was desperate enough to try. I went to my doctor who told me that if I was careful, I just *might* be able to fast. The key was careful control of my blood sugars. My doctor, a member of the Church, didn't encourage me or discourage me. It was my choice.

So after two years in my wheelchair, I fasted. I was hoping for a sudden healing. That didn't happen, but the Lord did soothe my heart and let me know that he was very much aware of me. His personal attention has sustained me through countless trials. I knew that my prayers *were* being heard and I would be healed and walk again (eventually). I believed in my future as a person who would walk again. From that hope and belief came the foundation of my faith.

Plain and simple, we live our faith by what we do. I have done my specific therapy exercises for at least two or three hours a day, six days a week, for the last four years. I have made significant progress in tiny, almost unnoticeable ways; I am definitely healing.

Living my faith means I am now walking 544 feet a day on my walker. I still need a helper who spots me because I sometimes tip over; but two years ago, no doctor even imagined I'd ever be using a walker at all. To walk from my front porch to my back door (136 feet), currently takes me an average of six minutes. When I first walked that distance, my average speed was twenty-seven minutes. I keep persisting, and that keeps me improving.

I had another very important experience with the Lord that taught me something I had never expected to learn about faith. One Sunday our Gospel Doctrine teacher mentioned a scripture that promised the Lord would heed our prayers when we repented.

Impressed and intrigued, I sincerely prayed to know what the Lord wanted from me. Finally after three weeks I received an answer that entirely surprised me. Unmistakably the Spirit told me I needed to go to bed earlier and get more sleep! After a few more days of pondering, wondering, and repenting, and being surprised at how hard it was for me to repent by going to bed earlier, I finally came to understand more exactly what it was the Lord wanted me to learn from going to bed by 10:30 P.M.

When I argued with him, telling him about all the good things I could accomplish (like writing in my journal and reading the scriptures) by staying up just a little later, he listened patiently and with love to my reasoning. But I could tell I still hadn't changed his mind.

The more I pondered this request to repent by going to bed earlier, the more I came to understand that the

Lord was simply asking me to trust him. Instead of taking everything on myself, and frantically trying to do it all—and staying up too late and getting up too early to do it—he simply wanted me to trust him. Let him find ways to accomplish the things that were physically impossible for me, or that were keeping me up too late. He simply wanted me to know he was in charge. Work hard at what I could do; *trust* him to help me somehow with the rest.

I have learned, whatever my problems may be, if I pray sincerely for his help and grace, turning my problems over to him—whatever I can't do that needs to be done, he *will* find a way to accomplish, if it truly needs to be done.

In the last eight years, I have lived through very many hard lessons. But my motto is "trust and relax in the Lord!"

And guess what? I'm still alive and still kicking!

The Fighter

S. E. KISER

I fight a battle every day
Against discouragement and fear;
Some foe stands always in my way,
The path ahead is never clear!

I must forever be on guard
Against the doubts that skulk along;
I get ahead by fighting hard,
But fighting keeps my spirit strong.

I hear the croakings of Despair,
The dark predictions of the weak;
I find myself pursued by Care,
No matter what the end I seek;

My victories are small and few,
It matters not how hard I strive;
Each day the fight begins anew,
But fighting keeps my hopes alive.

My dreams are spoiled by circumstance,
My plans are wrecked by Fate or Luck;

Some hour, perhaps, will bring my chance,
But that great hour has never struck;

My progress has been slow and hard,
I've had to climb and crawl and swim,
Fighting for every stubborn yard;
But I have kept in fighting trim.

I have to fight my doubts away
And be on guard against my fears;
The feeble croaking of Dismay
Has been familiar through the years;

My dearest plans keep going wrong,
Events combine to thwart my will;
But fighting keeps my spirit strong,
And I am undefeated still!

A Blessing in Disguise

MARILYNNE LINFORD

*T*he night before my scheduled shoulder surgery, with my right arm hanging limp at my side, my
husband and son-in-law gave me a blessing. The surgeon
guaranteed the operation would relieve the pain 100 percent but gave only a 50 percent chance of ever regaining
full use of my arm. The blessing promised a complete
recovery including the words "full range of motion."

Nearly five months passed during which I went to
therapy two or three days a week and did the prescribed
exercises at home on the other days. No matter how
hard I tried; I could move my arm only just above shoulder height—130 degrees. I desperately needed the full
180-degree range. I was confused. Perhaps the blessing
meant that 130 degrees with no pain was a complete
recovery; perhaps I just had to keep doing the exercises;
perhaps my full recovery would come in the resurrection. Without more range of motion and the strength
that would come with it, I couldn't do my household
work. I couldn't vacuum, clean a mirror, reach my head
to comb my hair, get dressed if there were buttons,

snaps, or zippers in the back, play the piano, carry a gallon of milk, or hold a grandchild.

Three days before Thanksgiving, I was with one of my daughters in a warehouse store. I turned a corner and fell over a forklift someone had left in the aisle, injuring my ankle. It was extremely painful. My daughter drove me to the clinic. The X ray showed no broken bones, but the ankle was badly sprained. The doctor wrapped my ankle and sent me home with painkillers and crutches. As I was wheeled to the car in a wheelchair, I wondered how I could possibly prepare Thanksgiving dinner for twenty with a weak shoulder restricting my mobility and a sprained ankle.

When we got home, my daughter brought the crutches to me so that I could get out of the car and into the house. When I tried to put the crutch under my bad shoulder, the pain was excruciating. My shoulder was so weak that I could not use the crutches! The only way I could get up the fourteen stairs and into the house was to crawl. Crawling hurt my shoulder and my knees but that pain was insignificant compared to the pain when I tried to use the crutches. With much help I got through Thanksgiving, crawling almost everywhere around the house. The first few days I just limped along like a wounded puppy, but as the days went on, I could crawl much better. The shoulder pain was almost gone.

In about ten days my ankle was well enough that I could hobble instead of crawl, and at some point, I realized that my right shoulder didn't hurt to use the crutch. I raised my arm to see how high it would go. To my total amazement, it was better—completely and absolutely better—180 degrees of motion plus the strength to lift a gallon of milk, vacuum, comb my hair, and carry sweet grandchildren. I chided myself for the negative thoughts and murmuring I had done. I thought the sprained ankle was the adversity wolf at my door adding the adversity of a sprained ankle to the adversity of a weak and immobile shoulder, when in actual fact, it was the miracle to heal my shoulder as the blessing had promised.

Battling On

ALISON HORROCKS FAIFAI

*A*s a very small child I didn't know my father was any different from other fathers. But as I grew older I began to wonder, and one day I asked him, "Dad, don't you ever wish you could run and jump and skip?" He looked at me and said, "This life is like a click of the fingers compared with all eternity, where I will be able to do those things that I am unable to do now."

My father, Harold Horrocks, of Auckland, New Zealand, never really knew good health. A doctor predicted he wouldn't live past forty. He lived forty-five years beyond that prediction, even outliving the doctor! Each second of each day was filled with pain from osteoarthritis. But this disability didn't prevent him from falling in love with and waiting ten years to marry my mother, Roma Tremain.

By 1945 Harold and Roma had two small children. Dad's health had so deteriorated that my parents lost count of the number of operations he had endured. He developed additional ailments but, in his own words, "battled on." After twenty-two years of work, he realized that he would not be able to continue his job at the Union Steam Ship Company, where he had worked as an accountant. In those days there was no government assistance. If you had no income, you had nothing. Father was determined to find a way to support his family. He bought opossum and sheep skins and laboriously cut and hand-stitched them, transforming them into stuffed rabbits, koala bears, lambs, and other sheepskin products to sell.

When a third child was on its way, my parents knew they needed more income to support their family. They decided to start their own home business, making children's clothing. Dad laid out the patterns, ordered, cut the fabric, and was the accountant. Mum was the supervisor, seamstress, and sales representative.

We were a religious family and prayed about our many challenges. The Lord heard our prayers and sent two missionaries. Father was seriously ill and bedridden, and Mother was at first reluctant to let the missionaries in. But they showed compassion for Dad's health problems and continued to drop by. Finally, Father said, "Who are those young men who are so interested in my health? Next time they call, invite them in."

Father's baptism was a test of faith. He was completely reliant on brethren who did not know how to assist him into the font and support him in the water. It was reasonable to fear that if they dropped him he could drown. But Father was filled with gratitude at the opportunity to become a member of The Church of Jesus Christ of Latter-day Saints.

The message of the restored gospel changed Father's perspective. He wanted to be obedient to every commandment. When he realized that keeping the business open on the Sabbath was violating a commandment, he closed the clothing factory on Sundays. Amazingly, the amount of work my parents accomplished in six days was equal to what they had accomplished in seven. They discovered tithing, and the windows of heaven were opened.

When the Auckland Stake was formed 18 May 1958, Dad was set apart as an assistant ward finance clerk. Mum was his caregiver, chauffeur, and legs. When Dad was called on an eighteen-month mission as finance secretary for the Auckland Mission, she was called as mission chauffeur to drive him to and from the mission home.

Father's greatest challenge came when he was called as bishop of the Auckland Third Ward. Father was beloved by the ward for many reasons; foremost being that during the five and one-half years as a bishop, he accompanied every member who attended the temple for the first time. This was no easy task. The New Zealand Temple is in Hamilton, a two-hour drive on bumpy roads from home. Later Father served as patriarch of the Auckland Mt. Roskill Stake for twenty years—until his death in 1993. He spent many hours as a two-finger typist transcribing the blessings he had given to stake members.

At fifty-six years of age Dad returned to work as an accountant. His new employer modified the workplace to accommodate his disability. He retired at sixty-five.

Dad attended night school and passed exams on radio transmission, his long-time hobby. He was unable to climb the stairs to the classroom, so my brother carried his frail body up and down the several flights of stairs.

While in his seventies, father purchased his first computer and entered all the family genealogy. Mum and Dad volunteered and drove "Meals on Wheels" to those in the community who were housebound or less able than themselves. Mum drove the car and delivered the meals and Dad was the map-reader and navigator. They were a team.

Father's testimony gave him power to cope with life on earth in a disabled body. When asked if he would like to live his life over again, he quoted the words of Winston Churchill: "Happy, vivid and full of interest as it has been, I do not seek to tread again the toilsome and dangerous path. Not even an opportunity of making a different set of mistakes, and experiencing a different series of adventures and successes would lure me. I am not so sure that I would do as well the second time as I did the first time through."

"There Are Many Things Worse than Cancer"

MARILYNNE LINFORD

From the day she arrived on earth (31 July 1956) to the day she departed (29 March 2000), everyone who knew Dixie Crystal loved her. Her life was full of fun, laughter, and unexpected surprises. She was innately happy.

Dixie was a watercolor artist and a creator of folk art, but most of all she was a costume designer. She could sew anything she saw in magazines or movies.

Though Dixie was never a bride herself, she made wedding dresses for anyone who asked. She did not need marriage to truly live "happily ever after." She found her happiness in service. The clock and the next day's workload meant nothing if she was involved in a creative project. She'd stay up half the night to finish a project for someone else.

She designed doll clothes for Marie Osmond and did costuming for television series such as *Touched by an Angel* and *Promised Land*. She became co-owner of Salt Lake Costume and found fulfillment in her gifts—

designing and making costumes at her own company. There was one unforeseen downside, however. Being co-owner of a small company meant that medical insurance was something she kept planning to get.

Before she found the lump—but not before she obtained health insurance—the depth of her character was evident, as was her love of life and service. But the Lord wasn't finished with her. She had a mastectomy in September 1998 and things looked good for a year. Then, the cancer raised its ugly head in her brain and bones. As the tumor wrapped around her spine, Dixie's mettle crystallized. She was often heard to say, "There are many things worse than cancer." Her faith and courage, her humor and charm, blossomed in adversity.

Because Dixie had no insurance, it was easy for others to answer the question "What can I do for Dixie?" Her neighborhood held a boutique as a fund-raiser, which contributed fifteen thousand dollars toward paying the bills. The day of the event pink ribbons for breast cancer awareness were tied on the trees and the lampposts in a nine block area. It made the evening news. Even the neighborhood children helped. A neighboring ward's Primary children donated money that had been budgeted for their quarterly activity day. Dixie hardly knew how to say thanks for those children and their eighty-eight dollars. On another occasion, some dear friends who owned a floral shop sent Dixie more than ten dozen roses of every shade and size possible.

As the doctors' appointments brought more and more bad news, Dixie found solace in spending time tending her nieces. She kept her journal faithfully as long as she could. She wrote: "This is a world in which we are to prove ourselves. The lifetime of a man is a day of trial wherein we may prove to God, in our darkness and our weakness where the enemy reigns, that we are our Father's friends and that we receive light from Him." Another journal entry was written on a Sunday evening after a Relief Society lesson had been on accepting changes in our life. She wrote, "We not only accept change in our lives, we should embrace our trials and dance with them and have others join with us so we can grow together. If that is the case, then I have a whole village dancing with me." Her motto came from an M. A. Marshall quote: "Courage doesn't always roar. Sometimes courage is the quiet voice at the end of the day; I will try again tomorrow."

Everyone faced with cancer has to make a decision to accept it and move on or just give up. Dixie accepted her future, knowing that it wasn't going to be easy. Through her whole ordeal, she kept a light heart and faced every setback with bravery. David, a brother expressed the family's love and admiration for Dixie with these words: "She left a footprint on each heart because she didn't let cancer rob her of anything. All that mattered she kept alive—her love, her hope, her faith, her sense of humor, her friendships, her memories, her eternal goals, her determination and courage, her beauty."

Who's in Charge?

CAROL BERNSTROM HOGLE

*J*ust before beginning my second year at the university, I met Hugh Hogle. The day following our first date, he told one of my sorority sisters that he had met the girl he was going to marry. Two months later we were married. We had four daughters and two sons. My husband and children were a great source of joy, learning, love, and happiness for me. I loved life and wouldn't have changed anything. I was in charge—and if I didn't know something, Hugh surely did. He finished medical school, an internship, and his residency. He began his general surgery practice in 1968, and life just kept getting better. Hugh loved life and what he was doing. But as the years wore on, his work, especially his work with breast cancer patients, slowly wore on him. His desire to serve made it hard for him to limit his practice or say *no* to anyone.

On 15 January 1995, when Hugh was fifty-six years old, he suffered a massive stroke on the left side of his brain. This paralyzed the right side of his body and took away his speech and his ability to read and write. In one blinding instant I realized that my life would never be the same again.

Just after the stroke, we moved into a new home. Our daughter Holly, who much to our horror had recently joined the LDS Church, said she thought it would be good if I found friends in this new neighborhood. She said the best place to become acquainted was at Relief Society, and she would go with me!

Since Hugh's stroke, Holly had talked to me about her faith and had often sent scriptures to me. I confess, the only reason I was willing to go to Relief Society that day was because I was grasping for anything that would make us the perfect family again. Before the stroke I was sure that I was a great mother, wife, and person and didn't feel a need for religion. Now, however, I began to feel that need. I needed answers. I began to realize that to gain back that perfect family, I must find out who was in charge of the world. Hugh wasn't in charge anymore—and I certainly wasn't. So who was? I needed to find out. Little by little as I went to church, studied the gospel, and prayed, I came to realize that this life is but a twinkling in eternity, and that the things that had brought me such pleasure, family and friends, were still there for me.

As I let the gospel into my life and began to realize the impact of family and friends, things changed. I am especially grateful for two friends, Valerie and Earl Parker, who worked with Hugh every day for nine months so that I could have a break.

My daughter Holly later confided to me that she sometimes wondered if the Lord had allowed the stroke to happen. Could this be true? Could there be blessings as a result of the stroke? Was the purpose to lead me to the gospel of Jesus Christ? If so, it certainly worked. Since my first week at Relief Society, I have not wanted to miss a single Sunday. I now teach Relief Society.

Once I let go of the awful burden I had placed upon my husband and myself to be perfect, I began to heal. I began to see that God does care about his children. I learned that sometimes he permits terrible things to happen to good people to make them better.

I now am able to celebrate the good in the world and refuse to concentrate on the bad. There are so many good people and so many good directions I can go. I look forward to each day and to each new experience. I am grateful for all I can do for Hugh. He is, as he was the day I met him, an extraordinary man. I thank the Lord for the things He has given me—two hands to help Hugh tie his shoes, the ability to read and share the written word with him, the ability to write and reply to the hundreds of encouraging words that have been written to him. I am grateful that I can pick up a phone and make a call for him because he can't. I am grateful for new technology and the ability to understand it and use it. Most of all, I am grateful for the atoning sacrifice of our Savior and his great love for me. Sometimes I allow myself to wonder if I would have ever found the gospel if it weren't for the stroke. I'm so much better off now. Though everything in our lives has changed, I am never alone. I know that believing Jesus Christ is the path to happiness in this life and to eternal life in the world to come. I thankfully acknowledge who really is in charge.

Bigger than the Mountain

CAROLYN M. PROBST

*W*hat do you do when you meet a mountain so high you can't climb over it, so wide you can't go around it, and so thick that you can't tunnel through it? Answer: make yourself bigger than the mountain. My husband, Brent, made himself bigger than his mountain.

At the time of Brent's diagnosis with multiple sclerosis, he was a devoted father of four—soon to be five—children, a businessman with a fledgling insurance business, and a counselor in the bishopric. We were devastated and heartbroken over this disease that had dared to interrupt our busy and happy life. In our despair and sorrow, we phoned family and friends to ask them to set aside a day of fasting and prayer on Brent's behalf.

On the day of the fast, Brent and I went to his former mission president, James A. Cullimore, to receive a priesthood blessing. I wept after the blessing because in it there was no mention that Brent would get well. We felt President Cullimore straining, yearning to proclaim a miracle, yet the inspiration of a promise of health did not come to him. I prayed quietly, hoping that we were deserving of a miracle.

Realizing my need, President Cullimore and his associate gave me a blessing for strength that the Lord would sustain me in supporting my husband during this challenge. We went to the Salt Lake Temple that day with heavy hearts, wondering what the future held for us and if we could measure up to it.

We carried with us a tremendous weight as we returned to our little starter home and our young children. But as we walked through the front door of our home, something changed. We were met with a great blast of warmth that both physically and spiritually calmed our souls. We looked at each other with an immediate understanding that the Lord was truly mindful of us and had sent his Spirit to comfort and strengthen us. From that day on, a beautiful spirit of peace and comfort has remained in our home.

The Lord with his mercy in effect said, "I won't take away your trial, but I will provide a way that you can endure it. You will have my Spirit with you." From that time on, we needed the Comforter in our home just as we needed electricity and water. We couldn't get along without it!

Brent's illness progressed—first a cane, then a wheelchair, and finally bed rest. Throughout his difficult life, he developed a profound positive attitude. This journal entry, from a particularly trying time of his life, illustrates his unwavering courage. "Six months after I broke my only useful arm, another tragedy happened and I broke my hip. I was now bedfast, unable to turn in my bed or care for myself. With nothing but time on my hands, I pondered just what my attitude could be. I determined then, that although I had lost control of my body functions, I had not lost control over my will, my soul, my thoughts. During this time I often recited to myself the words of the hymn by Will Thompson to keep up my courage.

> "Have I done any good in the world today?
> Have I helped anyone in need?
> Have I cheered up the sad
> and made someone feel glad?
> If not, I have failed indeed.
> (*Hymns,* no. 223)

"I pondered on the words of this hymn and realized that for years those words, which my Grandfather Richards had taught to me as a boy, had been my creed."

By focusing on the words of his favorite hymn, Brent served by doing immense genealogy and temple work. He didn't dwell on his illness; he lived above it. One evening, when Brent was very ill, our home teachers were visiting. One of our home teachers, Sam Plowgian, asked Brent a question, "Brent, do you ever ask the Lord why me? Why does this have to happen to me?" After a slight pause, Brent said in a humble, quiet voice, "Why *not* me?" We fell silent after such a profound statement.

Brent battled the effects of multiple sclerosis for a period of twenty-four years. After six years without use of arms or legs, Brent was rushed to the hospital, where his blood pressure and fever spiked regularly. The nurses reported that Brent was near death. During the long hours of the night, he had a sacred experience where he saw beyond the veil. He gained strength and courage from his solid testimony. Quoting from his journal:

"I know beyond a shadow of a doubt that we are placed here in our second estate for a specific purpose. At the time we were born, a very thick veil was placed over our minds. This was done so we would be forced to develop faith. I can tell you that sometimes this veil becomes very thin as I have experienced many times the thinning of this veil. I can only tell you that as we live our lives in harmony with the gospel teachings, the gift and power of the Holy Ghost will enable us to see more clearly along life's road. I bear my testimony that God does live and that his Son, Jesus Christ came to earth, lived his life, and paid the price for our individual salvation. I am grateful for his life and teachings. Some day we shall have the great privilege of meeting him and associating with him. What joy this will be for us!"

Thy Soldiers: Faithful, True, and Bold

True Courage

AUTHOR UNKNOWN

The wife who girds her husband's sword,
    'Mid little ones who weep or wonder,
And bravely speaks the cheering word,
    What though her heart be rent asunder,
Doomed nightly in her dreams to hear
    The bolts of death around him rattle,
Has shed as sacred blood as e'er
    Was poured upon a field of battle.

The mother who conceals her grief,
    While to her breast her son she presses,
Then breathes a few brave words and brief,
    Kissing the patriot brow she blesses;
With no one but her secret God to know
    The pain that weighs upon her;
Sheds holy blood as e'er the sod
    Received on freedom's field of honor.

Sergeant Bulletproof

KRIS MACKAY

$\mathscr{T}$hree nights before the United States entered the war in April 1917, George Hughes had a vision of himself as a soldier in a blue uniform. It wasn't a dream but an actual vision, a flash of foreknowledge, and he saw himself returning home alive. The next morning he related to his mother what he had seen, and on April 6 he enlisted in the Marine Corps, donning the very uniform that in the vision he had seen himself wear.

By early July he was sent overseas, and he ended up in Belleau Woods in France, on a wooded hill in a perfectly level area called Boursches wheat fields. He was attached to a regiment in the Second Division of the American Expeditionary Forces. His outfit helped stop the German army in its drive toward Paris.

George was very angry that day because many of his fellow soldiers and close friends had been shot. Down the hill he could clearly see lines of German soldiers bearing Maxim machine guns invented in the United States, weapons refused by the American military but used to terrible advantage by the enemy. Their guns were set up on tripods, and the tripods were so numerous that they touched each other for what seemed to stretch on for miles.

George was a sniper—a marksman who could hit a circle the size of a silver dollar at 500 yards, five times out of five. A telescopic sight on his rifle enabled him to blast small targets at far distances.

Just before dawn he secretly made his way to a sheltered spot where he expected to do some sniping. Crawling along the ground, he heard somebody cry for help. He stopped to listen, and decided the sound must have come from a shell hole down the hill and only ten yards in front of an active German machine gun nest. He pinpointed the distance by fire from the enemy guns.

He watched, his heart in his throat, wondering what to do, while rays of early morning sun lit up the white hand groping out of the hole, and again came that pitiful cry for help. He whispered to himself, "I'm sorry, soldier. We can't get you out of there. It's impossible." Then he felt a touch on his shoulder and heard a voice say, "Only you can, George. Only you."

George crawled back to Lieutenant Hal N. Potter and requested permission to attempt the rescue. The lieutenant refused. Anyone foolish enough to volunteer would be moving directly toward the murderous enemy guns, a perfect target. The attempt would be suicide.

George said, "Lieutenant, I'm telling you I *can* go get that soldier and come back." He was so insistent that against his better judgment the officer relented.

Word was passed along American lines that when Sgt. Hughes started down the hill, all guns were to fire as a diversionary action. He jumped out of the trench and jogged down the hill—and every enemy gun also opened up, including those in the forbidding nest closest to the soldier he hoped to reach.

He fixed his eyes on the point of fire and saw bullets streaking out of the guns. Lots of bullets. Headed straight for him. Peculiarly, not one of them touched his body. Strafing kicked up dirt and debris all around him, as if someone had trained a water hose onto a lawn covered with leaves.

George dropped into the shell hole. There, frighteningly still, lay the form of a boy with a bloody wound in his right leg, which had been wrapped with raw salted pork or sowbelly before the soldier passed out. George threw the unconscious man over his shoulder, climbed out of the hole and looked directly into the eyes of the enemy. He said, "Guten morgen. Wie Gehen Sie?" And laughed.

The Germans sat frozen at their guns as if they were paralyzed, while George scanned the area for a way back to his camp. The hill wasn't high, but the man on his back weighed at least two hundred pounds. George wasn't sure his legs could make it. Finally he spotted a kind of rivulet, made his way up that indentation, and with his free right hand balanced his weight against the dirt.

In eerie silence he struggled up the hill and reached the safety of the trenches. Two other men leaped up to pull the soldier off his back as George rolled over and screamed out, "Hit the deck!" Just as he dived to the ground, the Germans opened up again. Every machine gun in the vicinity shot at them. Unfortunately his two courageous helpers were wounded, but not fatally.

From then on George's buddies called him "Sgt. Bulletproof."

St. Crispian's Day Speech

WILLIAM SHAKESPEARE

Editor's Note: This speech from Shakespeare's play Henry V
*precedes the play's depiction of the battle of Agincourt (25
October 1415). Historically, though Henry's army was out-
numbered by almost 5 to 1, they were victorious in battle over
the French army, which lost more than 6,000 men. The
English lost fewer than 450 men. This speech, made by King
Henry V, is a rousing call to courage.*

If we are mark'd to die, we are enow
To do our country loss; and if to live,
The fewer men, the greater share of honour.
God's will! I pray thee, wish not one man more.
By Jove, I am not covetous for gold,
Nor care I who doth feed upon my cost;
It yearns me not if men my garments wear;
Such outward things dwell not in my desires:
But if it be a sin to covet honour,
I am the most offending soul alive.
No, faith, my coz, wish not a man from England:
God's peace! I would not lose so great an honour
As one man more, methinks, would share from me

For the best hope I have. O, do not wish one more!
Rather proclaim it, Westmoreland, through my host,
That he which hath no stomach to this fight,
Let him depart; his passport shall be made
And crowns for convoy put into his purse:
We would not die in that man's company
That fears his fellowship to die with us.
This day is call'd the feast of Crispian:
He that outlives this day, and comes safe home,
Will stand a tip-toe when the day is named,
And rouse him at the name of Crispian.
He that shall live this day, and see old age,
Will yearly on the vigil feast his neighbours,
And say 'To-morrow is Saint Crispian:'
Then will he strip his sleeve and show his scars.
And say 'These wounds I had on Crispin's day.'
Old men forget; yet all shall be forgot,
But he'll remember with advantages
What feats he did that day: then shall our names,
Familiar in his mouth as household words,
Harry the king, Bedford and Exeter
Warwick and Talbot, Salisbury and Gloucester,
Be in their flowing cups freshly remember'd.
This story shall the good man teach his son;
And Crispin Crispian shall ne'er go by,
From this day to the ending of the world,
But we in it shall be remembered;
We few, we happy few, we band of brothers;
For he to-day that sheds his blood with me
Shall be my brother; be he ne'er so vile,
This day shall gentle his condition:

And gentlemen in England now a-bed
Shall think themselves accursed they were not here,
And hold their manhoods cheap whiles any speaks
That fought with us upon Saint Crispin's day.

"Give Me Liberty
or Give Me Death!"

PATRICK HENRY

March 23, 1775.

No man thinks more highly than I do of the patriotism, as well as abilities, of the very worthy gentlemen who have just addressed the House. But different men often see the same subject in different lights; and, therefore, I hope it will not be thought disrespectful to those gentlemen if, entertaining as I do opinions of a character very opposite to theirs, I shall speak forth my sentiments freely and without reserve. This is no time for ceremony. The questing before the House is one of awful moment to this country. For my own part, I consider it as nothing less than a question of freedom or slavery; and in proportion to the magnitude of the subject ought to be the freedom of the debate. It is only in this way that we can hope to arrive at truth, and fulfill the great responsibility which we hold to God and our country. Should I keep back my opinions at such a time, through fear of giving offense, I should consider myself as guilty of treason towards my country, and of an act of disloyalty toward the Majesty of Heaven, which I revere above all earthly kings.

Mr. President, it is natural to man to indulge in the illusions of hope. We are apt to shut our eyes against a painful truth, and listen to the song of that siren till she transforms us into beasts. Is this the part of wise men, engaged in a great and arduous struggle for liberty? Are we disposed to be of the number of those who, having eyes, see not, and, having ears, hear not, the things which so nearly concern their temporal salvation? For my part, whatever anguish of spirit it may cost, I am willing to know the whole truth; to know the worst, and to provide for it.

I have but one lamp by which my feet are guided, and that is the lamp of experience. I know of no way of judging of the future but by the past. And judging by the past, I wish to know what there has been in the conduct of the British ministry for the last ten years to justify those hopes with which gentlemen have been pleased to solace themselves and the House. Is it that insidious smile with which our petition has been lately received? Trust it not, sir; it will prove a snare to your feet. Suffer not yourselves to be betrayed with a kiss. Ask yourselves how this gracious reception of our petition comports with those warlike preparations which cover our waters and darken our land. Are fleets and armies necessary to a work of love and reconciliation? Have we shown ourselves so unwilling to be reconciled that force must be called in to win back our love? Let us not deceive ourselves, sir. These are the implements of war and subjugation; the last arguments to which kings resort. I ask gentlemen, sir, what means this martial array, if its purpose be not to force us to submission? Can gentlemen assign any other possible motive for it? Has Great Britain any enemy, in this quarter of the world, to call for all this accumulation of navies and armies? No, sir, she has none. They are meant for us: they can be meant for no other. They are sent over to bind and rivet upon us those chains which the British ministry have been so long forging. And what have we to oppose to them? Shall we try argument? Sir, we have been trying that for the last ten years. Have we anything new to offer upon the subject? Nothing. We have held the subject up in every light of which it is capable; but it has been all in vain. Shall we resort to entreaty and humble supplication? What terms shall we find which have not been already exhausted? Let us not, I beseech you, sir, deceive ourselves. Sir, we have done everything that could be done to avert the storm which is now coming on. We have petitioned; we have remonstrated; we have supplicated; we have prostrated ourselves before the throne, and have implored its interposition to arrest the tyrannical hands of the ministry and Parliament. Our petitions have been slighted; our remonstrances have produced additional violence and insult; our supplications have been disregarded; and we have been spurned, with contempt, from the foot of the throne! In vain, after these things, may we indulge the fond hope of peace and reconciliation. There is no longer any room for hope. If we wish to be free—if we mean to preserve inviolate those inestimable privileges for which we have been so long contending—if we mean not basely to abandon the noble struggle in which we have been so long engaged, and which we have pledged ourselves never to abandon until the glorious object of our contest shall be obtained—we must fight! I repeat it, sir, we must fight! An appeal to arms and to the God of hosts is all that is left us!

They tell us, sir, that we are weak; unable to cope with so formidable an adversary. But when shall we be stronger? Will it be the next week, or the next year? Will it be when we are totally disarmed, and when a British guard shall be stationed in every house? Shall we gather strength but irresolution and inaction? Shall we acquire the means of effectual resistance by lying supinely on our backs and hugging the delusive phantom of hope, until our enemies shall have bound us hand and foot? Sir, we are not weak if we make a proper use of those means which the God of nature hath placed in our power. The millions of people, armed in the holy cause of liberty, and in such a country as that which we possess, are invincible by any force which our enemy can send against us. Besides, sir, we shall not fight our battles alone. There is a just God who presides over the destinies of nations, and who will raise up friends to fight our battles for us. The battle, sir, is not to the strong alone; it is to the vigilant, the active, the brave. Besides, sir, we have no election. If we were base enough to desire it, it is now too late to retire from the contest. There is no retreat but in submission and slavery! Our chains are forged! Their clanking may be heard on the plains of Boston! The war is inevitable—and let it come! I repeat it, sir, let it come.

It is in vain, sir, to extenuate the matter. Gentlemen may cry, Peace, Peace—but there is no peace. The war is actually begun! The next gale that sweeps from the north will bring to our ears the clash of resounding arms! Our brethren are already in the field! Why stand we here idle? What is it that gentlemen wish? What would they have? Is life so dear, or peace so sweet, as to be purchased at the price of chains and slavery? Forbid it, Almighty God! I know not what course others may take; but as for me, give me liberty or give me death!

In Front of the Firing Squad

KRIS MACKAY

$\mathcal{E}$lder Richard Blodgett . . . sat with elbows resting lightly on a table in the home of Brother and Sister Krebs in Wuppertal, Germany. . . .

Once a month this good brother and sister invited all twelve zone missionaries into their home for dinner—no small undertaking at best. Today was Thanksgiving, and they'd gone all out in a country that doesn't even celebrate Thanksgiving. . . .

The thing that puzzled Rick was why this good man and his petite wife went to so much trouble and expense. A warm meal for a pair of young men far from home was understandable. But monthly feasts for the entire complement of the zone? He asked about it. Instead of the expected answer, he was hit with [a] strange question: "How much do you love the people you serve?"

Rick considered it seriously. He believed he *did* love this people among whom he labored. He knew he'd grown very fond of them. He admired and respected the German population at large for the way they'd come out of two world wars with national pride intact, and for the

266

enormous suffering he knew they'd endured. The man posing the enigmatic question was certainly no stranger to pain or suffering. He was scarred and blinded by one of the war's incendiary bombs, and yet he, his wife and five children, grown now and on their own, continued year after year as stalwarts in the faith.

Silence fell between the two men. Both were lost in thought. At last Brother Krebs spoke. "Let me tell you a story," he said softly.

* * * * *

It was wartime. American missionaries had been pulled out of the country and went home to be drafted. Some of them returned, but this time they came as sworn enemies.

One former elder wasn't happy with the situation. A corporal with a reconnaissance group, he went out with small advance patrols to set up routes of attack. Streets of the towns were familiar to him; he'd tracted them out such a short while ago.

He was unhappy for another reason. He felt out of place among his comrades. The sergeant, particularly, was a new breed to him—burly, swaggering, contemptuous of signs of weakness in the men beneath him. And this boy who neither drank, smoked, nor caroused was definitely a thorn in the sergeant's side, a youth he felt personally committed to boost into manhood. The air between them was charged, just waiting for a showdown. The corporal bit his lip and reminded himself he owed allegiance to the uniform, if not to the man himself.

Using great restraint, he got by without direct

confrontation until the afternoon he watched a group of German citizens being rounded up for looting in a town the Allies had just taken over. There were strict rules against looting, but when people were starving, rules were hard to enforce.

The sergeant manhandled the group roughly. Suddenly, without thinking of the consequences, the corporal acted on impulse. He brushed his superior aside and with obvious joy and cries of recognition, threw his arms protectively around one aging gentleman.

The sergeant was furious. He grabbed the corporal's arm, yanked him aside, and growled angrily, "What do you think you're doing?"

"Sergeant, I don't expect you to understand, but I love this man. I was a missionary before the war, and I taught him the gospel. He was the only person I ever baptized. He's a good man!"

If the sergeant was furious before, he turned a livid purple now. To have his authority challenged in front of the other men was intolerable.

"Insubordination, Corporal?" he said with eyes narrowed. "This man was caught looting, and apparently you need a lesson in loyalty. Okay. Early tomorrow morning he will be shot—and you'll be doing the shooting!"

The young man's face turned chalky white but he didn't flinch. "No! I won't do it, Sarge," he said. "There's no way you can make me do it."

That did it. Regaining authority was the only thing important now. "Let me understand you, Corporal. Are you disobeying a direct command in time of war? If so,

it's my duty to remind you that that's an offense pun-
ishable by death. We're moving fast, and I'm the law out
here. We don't have time for a court martial. You have
until morning to make up your mind. At five in the
morning that looter will be staring down the muzzles of
a firing squad. You'll either be on the business end of a
rifle, or you'll be standing beside your friend. Take your
choice."

* * * * *

Brother Krebs paused in his narrative. . . . Then in a
trembling voice he continued.

"The frightened corporal bravely stood his ground.
The next morning he and his elderly German brother
stood side by side and were shot down together in a
lonely field not far from here.

"You ask me why I go out of my way to show affection for American missionaries? Brethren, that man was
my father."

Loyalty and Honor in the 442nd

CHIEKO N. OKAZAKI

When [my husband] Ed was a student at the University of Hawaii, he and many of his friends, also Japanese-American, were members of the ROTC. When the Japanese Imperial Air Force bombed Pearl Harbor and the United States entered World War II, the ROTC and all of the other military units in Hawaii were immediately mobilized as part of the Hawaii Territorial Guard. After enough regular army troops had arrived from the States, Major Frazier, a brawny career officer, called the Japanese-American ROTC cadets into a meeting and, weeping, told them they were being dismissed from the ROTC because their ancestry meant, to those in command, the possibility that they might be disloyal. He was of German ancestry, and he shared with them his own experience of humiliation and frustration during the injustices inflicted upon German-Americans during World War I. He also gave them wonderful advice: "Don't retaliate. Don't fight back. Don't do anything foolish. Don't make it easy for them."

Ed and his friends were heartsick. Ed respected his Japanese ancestors, but he was third-generation Hawaiian and his loyalties were with the United States. He and about three hundred of his friends drafted a petition to the military governor that said, in essence, "Please let us serve our country. If you can't trust us with rifles, let us form labor battalions and replace the city workers who are applying to work for the U.S. Engineers Department. We'll be happy to collect the garbage." . . .

Their request was reluctantly granted, and the VVV (Varsity Victory Volunteers) was formed. . . .

It took a year, but their efforts paid off. The record of the VVVs and the fact that the FBI gave the Japanese-American community of Hawaii a clean bill of health—there wasn't even one documented case of sabotage or disloyalty—meant that the military officials finally took positive action on the repeated petitions of the young Japanese-Hawaiian men to be allowed to serve in the military. A special combat team was formed, the 442nd Infantry, which eventually included 4,500 Japanese-Americans. Its motto was "Go for Broke." . . .

Those men had an indomitable spirit. They never lost sight of their goal—to prove their loyalty. When they were sent to Europe, they were part of the invasion of Italy and fought their way up the peninsula and into France (where Ed was wounded). There are always three regiments in a division. When one regiment attacks, the other two wait in reserve.

The 442nd was a self-contained regiment. . . . It was never held in reserve. Naturally, when the division

commander got the 442nd—the way Ed told the story—
he would say, "Oh, great! Now I've got some help." So
he would attack with one of his three divisions and with
the 442nd in the lead. When that section of the line was
secured, the division commander would rotate his attack
division to the rear to rest while one of the two divisions
in reserve came up to the front lines. The 442nd, meanwhile, would be assigned to another division, and the
division commander there would say, "Great, now I've
got some help!" And he'd attack with one of his divisions and with the 442nd in the lead. So those men were
constantly fighting on the front lines. Ed said, "That
was good. What we wanted was a chance to prove our
loyalty, and that gave us the chance." The 442nd had the
highest rate of casualties of any unit fighting in World
War II, and it also had the highest rate of decorations.

A Davao POW

RICHARD PATTERSON

$\mathcal{O}$n Thanksgiving Day 1942, twenty-year-old James Harris Patterson arrived in Manila with his United States Air Force squadron. In May 1943, the Japanese attacked the squadron's base at Del Monte and destroyed what few planes they had. Later, during a transport, in which Jim was taking part, the trucks were stopped by a blockage on the road. Japanese soldiers immediately swarmed the truck. Food was seized and the men were taken prisoners.

Once captured, the prisoners of war were stripped of their valuables and crammed into a small shack to await their fate. They were interrogated, moved to a temporary prison camp, and then to Davao Penal Colony, which had been used by the Philippine government to house hardened criminals who had life sentences. Davao was a prison within a prison, surrounded by snake-infested jungles and swamps. This was home for Jim for most of the three years and four months he spent as a POW.

Jim had been baptized a member of The Church of

Jesus Christ of Latter-day Saints when he was nine, but religion had not become important in his life. He did, however, possess a deep sense of honor and honesty. There were ten or so Latter-day Saints in Jim's area of the prison camp. This group would sneak out once a week to pray together. They knew if they got caught that they would suffer dearly. These prayer circles sustained Jim; but it was Christmas Day 1943 when Jim was born spiritually and patriotically.

On that Christmas morning, the Latter-day Saint POWs were permitted to gather for sacrament meeting. It was the first sacrament meeting the POWs had held and the first one that Jim had ever attended in his life. One of their group broke a cracker into pieces in a mess kit, blessed it, and passed it. After that, another soldier blessed the water in a canteen cup that was passed around this small congregation. As Jim partook of the cracker and the water, a tingling sensation came over his entire body and he burned from within. He felt the Holy Ghost enter his soul. He knew that the gospel of Jesus Christ was true. His testimony was born. He made a commitment with the Lord that if he got home safely he would be an active member of the Lord's church. The Lord fulfilled his commitment to Jim, and Jim, in turn, continues to fill his part of that promise made nearly sixty years ago.

Jim's patriotic feelings also deepened on this memorable Christmas day. After their brief sacrament meeting, the POWs joined another group for a Christmas program. Somehow, one of the soldiers had smuggled in an American flag and kept it rolled up in a blanket. As this group of physically pathetic POWs quietly sang "God Bless America," the blanket was unrolled to reveal the American flag. "It gave us the courage to go on," Jim recalls. "It gave us something to live for and a reason to live to return."

Jim was liberated 9 September 1945 and returned home a better American and Latter-day Saint. Shortly after his return he met Faye Richards; they were soon married in the Salt Lake Temple. Together they raised three daughters and two sons. In April 1988, Jim and Faye were called to serve a temple mission in, of all places, Manila, Philippines.

Opportunity

EDWARD ROWLAND SILL

This I beheld, or dreamed it in a dream:
There spread a cloud of dust along a plain;
And underneath the cloud, or in it, raged
A furious battle, and men yelled, and swords
Shocked upon swords and shields. A prince's banner
Wavered, then staggered backward, hemmed by foes.
A craven hung along the battle's edge,
And thought, "Had I a sword of keener steel—
That blue blade that the king's son bears,—but this
Blunt thing!" he snapped and flung it from his hand,
And lowering crept away and left the field.
Then came the king's son, wounded, sore bestead,
And weaponless, and saw the broken sword,
Hilt-buried in the dry and trodden sand,
And ran and snatched it, and with battle-shout
Lifted afresh he hewed his enemy down,
And saved a great cause that heroic day.

A Quiet Courage

FRANKLIN L. WEST

*O*ne of our seminary men came into my office about a month ago, very quietly. I was startled and thrilled to see him and almost shocked—Brother Reed Probst, formerly a seminary teacher at Bancroft, Idaho, and later at Hyrum, Utah. He had been serving for thirty-three months as a chaplain over in the Pacific Ocean, in the very heart of those heavy battles [of WWII]. . . . We chatted about his work and he was very modest about what he had been doing. He said that originally there were some fifteen chaplains in their division, and there were only four or five of them left. Of the ten or eleven that had gone, half of them had either been killed or had died due to sickness and disease. The other five or six had cracked up mentally; they couldn't stand the terrific strain, the emotional shock of the terrible things they were going through. He said: "I attribute the fact that I am alive and so well, to the fact that I have lived the Word of Wisdom. God has been very good and kind to me." [Brother Probst] had a few months of rest in this country before he would be sent back into the conflict, to that ministering work of love that these chaplains are to do.

I visited with him . . . the last time he was standing in President Widtsoe's office, and I noticed a fine little decoration on his uniform, and I asked him what it was, and very modestly he got his briefcase out and allowed me to read about two or three pages of typewritten material. What he had done had been witnessed and the authenticity certified by six people, and it said substantially this, that this man, under heavy enemy fire, from daylight until dark, bullets flying all about him, bombs exploding, soldiers being killed on all sides, quietly and effectively went about giving first aid, helping to bury some of the dead, listening and praying for those who were passing away in their last throes of death. All day long, absolutely unconscious of all that danger and hazard and gun fire and noise and confusion, he went about silently and quietly, administering those loving and tender words of kindness, and listening to the last words of these soldiers who were going to the Great Beyond. This happened not once, but on a second occasion, in another part of the war, he did that very same thing, indicating quiet bravery and heroism and simple devotion to duty.

I was proud to get a picture of four of our seminary men, all chaplains who met together in Italy, in a similar undertaking. And many of these boys were not drafted, they volunteered, knowing the great hazards of the work they were about to perform. You know, that is the very spirit of our gospel.

A Million-Dollar Wound

CHIEKO N. OKAZAKI

$\mathcal{D}$uring WWII, my husband] Ed was trained to detect and remove mines in the attack. Whenever the opposing army retreated, it would bury anti-personnel and anti-tank mines in the valleys between the rugged mountains where the traffic would naturally pass. The U.S. army couldn't advance until the mines were out of the way. Ed tells about crawling forward on his hands and knees in the dark, feeling ahead of him for the trigger wires sticking up above the ground. If he felt one, there was a way to jam a pin into the firing mechanism so it wouldn't explode. They would dig up the disarmed mine, and the tanks and infantry could pass. You can imagine what a dangerous job that was and how many men died disarming the mines.

On October 19, 1944, the 442nd was in France. The division they were with was attacking a little hill as part of a larger objective. A regiment of Texans had broken through the German lines but then had been pinned down and surrounded. The 442nd was assigned to rescue them. . . . Ed had been working all night with his squad to clear a mine field. It was raining. He'd slept for just a few minutes, leaning against a tree in his poncho. Just after dawn he got the message that the colonel needed someone to disarm a booby-trapped motorcycle.

Ed thought, "All of my men have worked all night, too. I'll go myself." He was slogging through the rain up the hill with seven other men when the first shell of the morning from the German side, a big 88 mm, came flying over their heads and exploded among them. Three were killed outright. Ed and the other four were wounded, and Ed was awarded the Silver Star. His citation reads as follows: "When Sergeant Okazaki and four other men were wounded by shrapnel . . . he dragged his companions to the safety of a building in the midst of the barrage and, despite his wounds, proceeded to render them first aid. When the aid men arrived and, discovering his bleeding arm, attempted to administer first aid to him he refused medical attention, insisting that he was not seriously wounded. It was not until the four other men had been treated that he consented to receive treatment himself. It was then discovered that he had received three wounds—one in his arm and two in his left leg. Sergeant Okazaki's conspicuous courage, utter disregard for personal safety, and determination were an inspiration to the men of his company."

Ed jokes about his "million-dollar wound," saying it got him out of the war. But it took him a year in the hospital to recover. I often think what a miracle it was that he survived. More than that, it was a miracle that he survived with his gentleness, his kindness, and his good humor intact.

The Source
of a Convert's Courage

KARL R. KOERNER

$\mathcal{E}$lder Turner sat in the mission president's office explaining to the president why he thought Brother Chung-jui Chang should be baptized even though he was entering the Taiwan Army in less than two months. They both knew how hard it would be to maintain activity and a testimony during the two years of military service required by all healthy young men on the island. There would be no way to attend church on a regular basis, no way to observe the Sabbath day, and no relief from an environment that in many ways is contrary to what the Church teaches.

Chung-jui, however, had thoroughly investigated the Church for several years and felt it to be true. The gospel had brought purpose and meaning into his life when a close friend passed away. Elder Turner knew that Chung-jui was ready to make promises and commitments to God and change his lifestyle. He was ready for baptism.

As a new member, Chung-jui went in the army. It was

a spiritually discouraging environment. Daily activities that he had started to take for granted were now impossible—going to church, kneeling in prayer, reading the scriptures. The language of many of his fellow soldiers was filthy, and they were always trying to involve him in their weekend jaunts to party, gamble, and carouse with women in town. He was so grateful for the protection his baptism offered. His sins of the past were a thing of the past and he wasn't about to go with these men and turn his back on his newfound faith.

One day, however, some of the men in the barracks were particularly demanding. "We're a unit, a team," they said. "It's only proper that you come loosen up with us." As usual, Chung-jui politely refused. Off the soldiers went. Later that night, when the men returned, five or six of them went over to Chung-jui's bed and forcefully pulled him out. They dragged him to a nearby field and started to rough him up. These were people he had thought were his friends. Why were they doing this? They beat him and cursed him. They drew their bayonets and guns and threatened to kill and bury him on the spot. One of them even had a shovel. "Why do you reject us? Are we really that bad? Is it really worth losing your life to not go out and drink beer with us? Don't be so stupid. You make the choice—from now on, are you going to come with us or not?"

How could this be happening? Chung-jui had never been so scared. He said a prayer in his heart, hoping the Lord would intervene in this terrible moment. As he prayed for courage, he knew what he had to do. A feeling of calm came over him and he began to draw strength from his faith in the Savior. "It is you who have the choice," he said. "You can kill me or not, but I have promised God I will not go with you to do the things you do and I cannot break that promise. I do not fear your knives and guns." With resolve in his voice and peace in his heart, he stood up to the men.

They angrily eyed Chung-jui and then looked at each other. Would they follow through on their threat? After what seemed like forever, their leader said, "Let him go." There was no response. "Let him go," he insisted. "Can't you see this man is braver than all of us? Do you not worry that if you kill this righteous man, God will bring his punishment upon our heads?" His face, barely visible in the darkness, was livid. "Put your weapons down or this man's blood will always haunt you." One by one, the soldiers loosened their grip and released Chung-jui.

It was not surprising that the next few months were accompanied by strained feelings in the barracks. But then something happened that was a surprise and shock to Kai-Ming. One of his attackers came to him and asked if he could know more about his church. "I'll never forget your courage," he said. "You were willing to give your life for what you believe. I need to know what gave you that kind of strength." Over the next few months, others also approached him to know more about his beliefs. In all, four of the men who attacked him that night eventually joined the Church. They found through personal experience that the gospel of Jesus Christ is not something you just learn about, it is something you live.

"That Mad Englishwoman"

CAROL R. GRAY

$\mathscr{F}$ive years ago, the war in Bosnia was raging. Living in England, details of the conflict bombarded us via television all the time. . . . As the ward Relief Society president, I wanted my sisters involved in a [service] project that would bless the lives of many. We decided on an appeal for aid to send to the people of Bosnia. Within three weeks of starting, it grew from a ward appeal, to a stake, to a city, and then to an area appeal. Thirty-eight tons of aid were collected. Imagine your stake's cultural hall covered from floor to ceiling with donations—that's about thirty-eight tons. . . .

To deliver our donations, I had arranged with an established London charity that went regularly into Bosnia and Croatia. I had no intentions of accompanying our shipment even part way or going near a war zone myself. I have seven children and a wonderful husband. I am not a kamikaze housewife. I planned to collect the donations and let the sisters lose themselves in the service of others, which they did admirably.

Two days before we were to transport all of our aid to

the London charity, they rang me and said, "Carol, we are really sorry, but we have run out of money. We can't take your aid." Everything we had gathered was stored in our ward meetinghouse. My bishop was sitting on diapers and milk formula. The family history center was closed because it was full of donations. . . . We did manage to move all the donations just in time to have sacrament meeting. I assured the bishop the meetinghouse would be clear by the next Sunday.

But now I had no means of transport. I was in an almighty mess. . . . I decided I had to deliver the donations to Bosnia myself. Drastic measures had to be taken. I sold my beautiful sports car and bought a twenty-eight-foot truck. . . . Many wonderful families joined with me, and we took 110 vehicles in all to transport our aid into Bosnia, a five-thousand-mile round-trip journey through Europe and the Balkans.

To go into these war zones was a big decision for me. . . . I drove along with my parting promise to my husband ringing in my ears: this will be a one-time thing, an adventure of a lifetime. I will do my bit, and I will never, ever do it again. We went through minefields, under shellfire and sniper fire, and my stomach dragged along the floor as we went. I would never in a million years have thought Carol Gray, a sister who had never gone to the temple without her husband, could do this thing. . . .

During that first convoy, I looked at those people, the devastation, and the nightmare that they were going through, and I knew that I had to return. I was overcome with the desire to help people. I knew that my

Heavenly Father had gotten me into something that I wasn't, after all, going to be able to turn away from easily.

Now, I have a husband in a million; he gives me lots of space to be who I am. But how was I going to explain to him when I got home that I needed to go again? When I arrived home from that first trip, I ran down the steps and threw myself into his arms. I didn't say a word, and he said, "I know. Don't tell me. You have to go back." That was thirty-one convoys ago. It's amazing how the Lord gets you to do things bit by bit.

In those early days, we took in hundreds of thousands of food parcels to all the families around the front line areas. I chose to go to front lines because the families there were in desperate need, and yet no charities were going to them. I was naive; they were front-line areas because they were surrounded by minefields and were constantly being shelled. No wonder no one would go there. Nevertheless, we went in, prepared by our fasting, prayers, and blessings, and we were safe. These areas aren't as dangerous anymore. The shelling has stopped—but the need is still desperate.

When the war was at its very worst, our food and medical supplies kept those people alive. We equipped the hospitals on the frontline with antibiotics, burn packages, and open-wound dressings. We kept those hospitals going, and it was a privilege. Now I'm involved with the rebuilding and re-equipping of schools, old people's homes, and medical centers, and supplying other desperately needed services.

I know that Heavenly Father opened doors that I

couldn't have opened and that he stood by our side many times when we were in dangerous situations. Once I hadn't rung my husband for five days. . . . I couldn't get to a phone because I was in a ravaged front-line area. Finally I was allowed to use a field phone that belonged to a doctor. . . . I rang my husband, "Hello, love, it's me. I'm fine." Suddenly there was the whine and loud thud of an incoming shell, followed by a large cloud of dust and rubble and searing heat and flames. We were cut off. No doubt my poor husband wondered if I had been blown up. I managed to get to another phone twenty-five kilometers down the road to call him back with reassurances. . . .

Who is the Lord going to use to help those who can't help themselves? Can he use those who can't even lift themselves up? Who does he need? He needs you and me, people who can go out and do. Service is wonderful, no matter where we serve. Not everybody is as balmy as I am and goes into a war zone. I've got a nickname with the personnel at all the borders. I'm "that mad Englishwoman." Five years ago, if you told me that I'd be doing what I'm doing, I would have thought *you* had gone quite mad. I'm not special. I'm just a very ordinary English sister that happened to get involved.

Memorial Day

EDGAR A. GUEST

These did not pass in selfishness; they
    died for all mankind;
They died to build a better world for all
    who stay behind;
And we who hold their memory dear,
    and bring them flowers to-day,
Should consecrate ourselves once more
    to live and die as they.

These were defenders of the faith and
    guardians of the truth;
That you and I might live and love, they
    gladly gave their youth;
And we who set this day apart to honor
    them who sleep
Should pledge ourselves to hold the faith
    they gave their lives to keep.

If tears are all we shed for them, then
    they have died in vain;

If flowers are all we bring them now,
    forgotten they remain;
If by their courage we ourselves to
    courage are not led,
Then needlessly these graves have
    closed above our heroes dead.

The Youth of Zion

Proud to Be a Mormon

VICTOR W. HARRIS

A close friend of mine once visited a rival high school. She was there to participate in an athletic contest as a cheerleader. As she and her friends got off the bus, they were greeted by a crowd of taunting students who abused them with profanity. Offended by the inappropriate use of the Savior's name, my friend demanded that they cease such language. This provoked one young man to taunt her even more with his profane language until, finally, she could take no more of it. She instinctively turned around and kicked him as hard as she could! When she demanded again that he cease such language, he yelled, "What are you, a Mormon or something!" She replied, "Yes I am, and I'm proud of it, too!" Others cheered her courage and began jeering the young man with the foul mouth. He eventually begged her pardon and finally admitted that he was a Mormon too. She then replied, "Well, then, why don't you act like it!" I'm not suggesting that we kick everyone who uses profanity, but there are many times when we must stand tall and make moral choices that are not easy to make.

"A Great Teenage Girl"

MARGARET D. NADAULD

I know of a young woman who lives in the United States. She was working with the Personal Progress program and, as one of her goals, wrote that she wanted to live worthy to be married for time and all eternity in the holy temple of God. Then, as we do in the Personal Progress program, she talked with her mother about her goal, even though her mother was not active in the Church. Susan's mom didn't say very much to her, but in her heart she too set a goal. The goal was that she, herself, would work to be married in the temple and sealed for time and all eternity to her family. There was one major problem (besides her inactivity). The problem was that her husband, Susan's father, wasn't a member of the Church. One day, when the time was right, Heavenly Father gave Susan's mom the courage to tell her husband about their daughter's goal of a temple marriage and about her own goal. Do you know what happened? The father said, "Well, if that's the case, I guess we'd better invite the missionaries over so I can find out what this church is all about!"

The rest of the story is that Susan's father was baptized and her parents were sealed in the temple, with their children. What a miracle! And all because of the courage of a great teenage girl.

Courage in a
Movie Theater Lobby

DIANE BILLS PRINCE

*A*ngie and her date arrived at the theater with the two other couples in their group. They found good seats inside and made themselves comfortable. Angie was having a great time until the movie began. Everything was all right for a while, but suddenly some scenes came up on the screen that made her feel extremely uncomfortable, scenes she knew she should not be polluting her life with. She turned to her date and whispered that the movie was making her uncomfortable and that she would wait in the lobby for him and the others. Then she had the additional courage to quietly get up and walk out by herself.

In the lobby, Angie was at peace inside. As embarrassing as it had been for her to get up and leave, she knew she had done the right thing.

Within a very short period of time, her date joined her in the lobby. He told her how proud he was of her for having the courage to get up and leave. They would wait together for the others. It wasn't long until couple number two joined them, and shortly couple number three came out of the theater as well. Because one young woman chose to follow the light of the Spirit inside of her, she became an example to others.

An Alternate Assignment

JOAN B. MACDONALD

One of my friends has a teenage daughter, Jenny, who has great faith and a strong testimony. During her junior year in high school, her English class was asked to read a book that was filled with foul language. This young girl was soon deeply offended by what she was reading. She agonized over what she should do. She discussed the problem with her parents. Finally, she approached her teacher. She carefully explained her beliefs, explaining that she couldn't read the book in good conscience. Arrangements were made for her to read *The Taming of the Shrew* instead. The reading was more difficult. Furthermore, she lost the benefit of class discussions relating to the book she was reading, resulting in a grade that was lower than usual. Nevertheless, Jen was glad she had made the choice she had. The process taught her several important lessons: She learned she had a choice. She learned what she wanted her choice to be. She learned she was capable of defending her faith to an adult authority figure. Perhaps most important, she learned she was a young woman of conviction and courage. A year later, when Jen was applying for admission to Brigham Young University, her English teacher wrote a letter of recommendation for Jen in which she recounted this story, praising Jen for her integrity. Jenny will never forget this experience. It strengthened her testimony, deepened her faith, and increased her courage.

Before the Moment of Crisis

ED AND PATRICIA PINEGAR

A young boy . . . early in his life had made a promise to God that he would never do anything to hurt his mother. Later, after he had grown older, he . . . made another promise that he would never do anything to offend God. Armed with that dual determination he was eventually confronted with a significant temptation.

His high school football team had won a game, and the players and some other fellows had gathered at a house where they were basking in the joy of victory. When one of the boys asked if he could have a drink of water, the host of the party invited him to help himself. Opening the kitchen cupboard to get a glass, he noticed a bottle of cooking wine on a shelf.

"Hey, you guys. Look what I've found! It's almost full! Let's see what wine really tastes like."

With their curiosity aroused and being in a jubilant mood, many of the boys exclaimed, "Yeah, let's do it!"

Only one boy expressed any reservation. "Hey, guys, we shouldn't do this. It isn't right, and besides, the wine isn't ours. You know darn well we shouldn't do this."

Then the abuse began. "What are you, a goody-goody? Hey, flake off, man. We don't need you telling us what to do."

The young man now had to make a decision. "If I drink it, I'll be their pal. If I don't, they'll make fun of me."

Just then he noticed a boy standing in the doorway. The boy was younger, a deacon in the ward where he was a priest. Recalling the promises he had already made—to his God and to his mother—the older boy put his arm around the younger boy's shoulders and said, "Come on, we don't belong here." They walked away with taunts ringing in their ears but feeling satisfied that they had chosen to do what was right.

You have to wonder what the outcome might have been had the priest not internalized his values and made a decision prior to the temptation—before the moment of crisis.

"She's a Mormon, and She Doesn't Drink"

BARBARA LEWIS

$\mathcal{T}$allee's reputation for fighting substance abuse spread through the high school, and she influenced other students. For example, one evening at a party someone asked her if she wanted a drink. From the other room, a guy yelled, "Don't ask her. She's a Mormon, and she doesn't drink."

"Don't push her," another boy said. "If she drank anything . . . Well, I'd be . . . sort of disappointed."

At a beach party one of the most popular girls came up to Tallee and asked, "Would you be disappointed in me if I drank?"

Tallee answered, "You have the right to choose what you want to do. Everyone has that freedom." The girl smiled, and Tallee couldn't help but notice that her friend didn't drink all that night. With Tallee's encouragement, two young men also stopped drinking completely. . . .

One summer, Tallee went to Villennes, France, for one month as a foreign exchange student. The first night she attended a yard party with some students who were celebrating passing a major exam. A few parents and even some teachers were there. They surrounded Tallee and tried to encourage her to taste the wine.

"Try some of this wine. It is the best in the world."

"No, thank you," Tallee struggled with French. "I'd like the juice, please."

"A little wine is good for you. It aids the digestion."

"It's the water that is unhealthful." They all laughed.

She looked around the table at their smiling faces and felt strange with her glass of orange juice. Fearful that she was offending them, she wondered if she should pretend to drink some of the wine. It was so hard to explain in French.

"Here try this, my dear. This is the best of the vine."

Tallee wondered if she could keep saying "no" anymore. She silently prayed that she could be strong, and then almost miraculously, they quit asking her. This happened several times. Each time that Tallee felt herself weakening under the pressure, she prayed for strength, and they quit asking her to take a drink.

That night she got on her knees and thanked her Father in Heaven that he hadn't let her be tested beyond what she was capable of handling. "I realize now, Father, that when I'm trying to do what is right, you will protect me. You can help me overcome anything I need to. You have helped me regain my hands and have shown me how I can serve with them."

Helping Hands and Paws

C. TYLER BRIGGS

$\mathcal{O}$n 26 June 1981, I came to earth with congenital muscular dystrophy, a disability that has twisted my arms, hands, and legs, leaving me with very little use of the muscles in those limbs.

Despite predictions that I would not survive in this life, I was able to leave the hospital and go home with my mom and dad when I was three months old. For nineteen years my parents have literally served as my helping hands. As I grew, my legs and feet were fitted for braces. This allowed me to walk around the house as long as Dad or Mom held me under my arms. When there was no one to hold on to, I would pull myself around the house by lying on my back, arching my neck, and using my feet to push myself backwards. Slowly I gained mobility.

Then one day I pulled myself into my room using the arched-neck method. I slithered up the side of the bed, locked my braces, and used the wall to hold me up until I made it into the kitchen. Once I got to the kitchen, I stepped away from the wall, got my balance, and walked on the linoleum.

As my ability to move around improved, my parents searched for other ways to ease the pains and burdens that come along with my disability. They were referred to an excellent specialist in orthopedic surgery. This doctor used his hands to help mine. He straightened my wrists—which were positioned at a ninety-degree angle—and then proposed transferring a muscle from my back to my arm to give me a bicep. There were risks, but I was willing to try.

After many weeks of therapy and another operation to put my arm at a better angle, I was indeed able to bring my hand to my mouth. I was absolutely elated with the new independence. I could feed myself, type faster, and lift a cup off the table to take a drink. After seeing how well one arm worked, I had surgery for the other a couple of years later.

The summer before entering seventh grade I went to California to attend the Canine Companions for Independence (CCI) program to receive my golden retriever, Hedgecock, who is also my newest set of helping hands—or paws. Hedgecock gets my clothes, pushes elevator buttons, picks up things I drop, and gives my wallet to cashiers at the store.

Hedgecock has accompanied me to many events and activities throughout the years. One of our most exciting outings was to the Sterling Scholar assembly during my senior year of high school.

At the assembly the Sterling Scholar coordinator announced the recipient of the Accolade Award. But she had a surprise: "We are awarding two Accolades today because where you see one, you see the other. It is my profound honor to give Accolades to Hedgecock and to his master, Tyler Briggs."

The students in the audience jumped to their feet in applause. I started towards the podium and at that moment my counselor brought Hedgie on stage and presented him with a two-foot long rawhide bone with a bow tied around it. I cannot take credit for this award. I never would have succeeded without those many helping hands that instilled in me a belief that I could succeed. I am humbled to know that so many people believe in me. I am now at a new beginning. I am serving a mission as a family history specialist and hope to attend law school and become an attorney.

I'm grateful for everything my parents have done for me. I'm grateful to my surgeons and therapists. I'm grateful for my set of helping paws. The most important thing I've learned, however, is that God has blessed me with all that I have and am. I know without a doubt that he loves me. This knowledge is what gives me the drive to make the best out of every single day.

Aimee Walker:
An Olympic Hopeful

MARILYNNE LINFORD

𝒜imee Walker is a seventeen-year-old world-class gymnast, who hopes to be on the United States Olympic team in 2004. This is a courageous goal for anyone. For Aimee—who is blind in one eye, deaf, and was born without hip sockets, making it necessary to wear a brace until the sockets formed when she was one-and-a-half years old—the goal is particularly bold.

Aimee's silent world makes the floor routine especially difficult. She can't hear the music blaring over the loud speakers, so Aimee's coach selects a piece of music for the routine and turns up the volume all the way. Aimee places her hands on the speakers and feels the beat through them. Then she counts the rhythm as she learns the dance. When she performs, one of her teammates will mark the time for about ten seconds, then give the "go ahead" signal. More often than not Aimee comes in right on beat without ever hearing anything. Her teammates move to the corners of the mat so that when Aimee finishes a tumbling run, she can look up at them and find the beat again.

Aimee also has problems with the balance beam. Because she is blind in one eye, she has difficulties with the depth perception needed to maintain her balance. But with persistence, patience, and practice, she has learned to make mental and physical adjustments during her routine, learning each move through trial and error. Aimee feels these gifts are her opportunity to show other disabled young people that there is no limit to what can be achieved.

As an Olympic hopeful, Aimee had a spiritual experience that has given her courage and strength in her gymnastics career. "I had been working really hard to [qualify for the Senior International Elite Competitions,]" she begins. "Just before the meet, my dad called and said it was time for prayer. He said he had found a scripture that was written just for me and just for this occasion. He read Doctrine and Covenants 84:88: 'And whoso receiveth you, there I will be also, for I will go before your face. I will be on your right hand and on your left, and my Spirit shall be in your hearts, and mine angels round about you, to bear you up.' I read it again and again. It gave me confidence.

"All my [gymnastic] events went well until I got to the last event: the beam. I started to focus and think. This was my last event. I knew I had done well, but I couldn't fall off the beam. I thought of the scripture. In the middle of my beam routine, my worst fear happened. My foot slipped and I felt my body tipping and I couldn't get my balance. I was falling. Suddenly I could feel hands I couldn't see pushing and straightening me back up. The hands supported and steadied me, on my left and on my right. I was so excited and thankful. I cried at my dismount but gave the judges my biggest smile. I passed!

"The [second round] also went well. I did great on all my events. Then there was the beam again. I mounted, everything was perfect, but then on an easy trick, I fell. But I heard the voice of the Spirit telling me to do my best and everything would be all right. I dismounted and smiled for the judges. I was so nervous but I knew I had done my best. I sat waiting while the judges talked. They told my coach that I didn't make it. I thought, *Hey, it's okay,* but I cried. *Jesus is my example and with him I can get through anything.* My coach walked back over to the judges and they told her that they had made a mistake. I *had* made it! I was the only one from my team who passed 'senior international elite.' I had qualified to advance to the first of the three Olympic trial competitions—the U.S. Classic."

Aimee trained as hard as she could for the next round of competitions. During a practice, though, she sustained an injury after attempting a difficult trick on her floor routine. "I asked my dad and my grandpa to administer to me," she remembers. "Grandpa gave the blessing, which included this sentence, 'You will be able to compete and you will be an influence for good.' I believed those words but didn't know how it could happen. The Spirit told me not to worry.

"We flew to Oklahoma for the U.S. Classic. All the Olympic hopefuls were there. I told the team doctor how much I wanted to compete, but I was afraid of permanent damage to my knee. He cleared me for only one event—the bars. He taped, braced, and bandaged my knee. I did well, but I couldn't qualify with only one event. I had competed, though, fulfilling part of my blessing. I was confused about the second promise in the blessing, though. How could I be an influence for good when I didn't make it to the Olympics?

"As Mom and I were on our way out of the gym, the Fox Family Channel stopped us and said they were doing a documentary on the U.S. gymnasts. They wanted to include a segment about me! Why me? I only competed in one event and didn't win. They interviewed me; I didn't think much would come of it. But when the documentary aired, my story was featured throughout the whole two-hour special! The program concluded with my dismount from the bars and the narrator said, 'Because of a knee injury Aimee Walker will not be able to compete in the Olympics this year, but her hopes are high for Athens 2004.' The blessing was exactly fulfilled."

Saving a Friend

ARDETH G. KAPP

$\mathscr{F}$ollowing a talk at a youth conference, after everyone had shaken hands and few people were still around, I noticed one young woman standing some distance away. She had been waiting for a moment when she might speak with me in private. Together we moved away from the others into the seats near the rear of the chapel. The young woman, who was about fifteen, was serious and thoughtful. "I have a friend who is in bad trouble," she said. "She really needs help. What can I do?"

"Does your friend know that you know about her problem?" I asked.

"Oh, yes, she knows, but she would kill me if she ever thought that I told on her."

"How badly do you want to help her?" I asked.

"Well, somebody has to help her or she's going to make things even worse," she explained, "but what can I do? I'm not going to tell on a friend."

I was impressed with her sense of loyalty and her commitment to keep a confidence, but it was obvious that she also felt some responsibility for her friend, who was apparently in deep water over her head and perhaps even drowning. . . .

"You are carrying a tremendous responsibility on your young shoulders," I explained. "You need help because the weight will increase as you see your friend losing ground. I recommend that you seek help for yourself. Do you have a chance to talk to your bishop?" I asked.

"Sometimes," she said.

"Would you feel comfortable calling him and just telling him you have something you'd like to talk to him about?"

"Oh, I've never called the bishop. I don't know."

I realized that it would take a bit of courage for a young woman to call and make an appointment with her bishop, especially if she hadn't already had an opportunity to become friends with him. Her hesitation prompted another approach.

"How would you feel if I called and made an appointment with your bishop for you?"

"What would you say?" she asked. "I don't want the bishop to think I'm in trouble."

"I would assure him that you are not in trouble, but that you have a heavy responsibility and that you are striving to be a saint, a true disciple of our Heavenly Father. I would tell him that you want to be a true friend and to do only what is right, and you need his guidance. Now, you could talk to your parents or your friends or others, but the reason to call the bishop is because he is the one who can best help in times of serious problems, and you have a serious problem—a friend in desperate need of help."

Together we agreed that I would call the bishop and make the appointment for her. . . .

Two weeks later I received a telephone call. It was the young woman who was concerned about her friend.

"Do you have a minute to talk?" she asked.

"I sure do," I said, anxious to get a report concerning the heavy responsibility she was carrying.

"Well," she began in a happy voice, "I talked to my bishop, and he really understood. He really wanted to help, and he didn't ask me to tell on my friend. He just asked if I thought my friend would come with me to visit with him sometime that week." . . .

She paused a moment, then continued. "We went to the bishop's office. It was kind of scary at first, but I knew we were doing the right thing. As soon as we walked in, the bishop shook hands with each of us. He was so warm and friendly, like nothing was the matter. Then he sat down beside us and began to tell us, without mentioning any names, the concern he has for some of the youth in our ward. When we looked into his eyes, we could feel his love for them and for us too. It was like he really cared. It was more like talking to a friend than talking to the bishop. . . .

"When we were ready to leave, the bishop thanked us for coming in, and he told us that if we ever wanted to talk to him again or alone, he would be happy to spend some time with us. My friend was . . . crying. 'Would you like to talk to the bishop alone?' I asked her. She nodded her head. The bishop gave me a copy of the *New*

Era and asked me to wait in the chapel while they talked. I sat there in the chapel waiting and praying that my friend would be able to tell the bishop all the things she had told me so that she could get the help she needed and so I wouldn't have to carry the load of knowing her problems all by myself. It seemed like she was there for quite a while, but I didn't mind waiting. I knew someone had come to the rescue of my friend. It was like Heavenly Father was there with us, and everything was going to work out if we worked together." . . .

I asked, "And how do you feel?"

"Wonderful," she said. "I feel that I have helped save my friend."

Sources and Permissions

Be Strong and of Good Courage

"'Let Me Be Brave in the Attempt'" by Jack R. Christianson, from "Parents: Builders of Men and Women," in *Eternal Families,* ed. Douglas E. Brinley and Daniel K Judd (Salt Lake City: Bookcraft, 1996), 248–50.

"Motherhood: The Greatest Career" by Linda J. Eyre, from *A Joyful Mother of Children* (Salt Lake City: Deseret Book, 2000), 123–26.

"The Missing Shoe" by Marvin J. Ashton, from *The Measure of Our Hearts* (Salt Lake City: Deseret Book, 1991), 96–97.

"I Wish You Could Know That Kind of Joy" by Kathleen H. Barnes, from "Letting the Light within Shine Forth," in *Arise and Shine Forth: Talks from the 2000 Women's Conference* (Salt Lake City: Deseret Book, 2001), 275–77.

"Courage" by Grantland Rice, in *Best-Loved Poems of the LDS People,* ed. Jack M. Lyon, Linda Ririe Gundry, Jay A. Parry, and Devan Jensen (Salt Lake City: Deseret Book, 1996), 44.

"Seeking the Will of God: Bit by Bit by Bit" by Pam Kazmaier, in *Hearts Knit Together: Talks from the 1995 Women's Conference,* ed. Susette Fletcher Green, Dawn

Hall Anderson, and Dlora Hall Dalton (Salt Lake City: Deseret Book, 1996), 66–73.

"Old Temple Shoes" by David C. Gaunt. Previously unpublished.

"Lessons Learned from Uncle Teddy" by Lowell L. Bennion, from *The Best of Lowell L. Bennion: Selected Writings 1928–1988,* ed. Eugene England (Salt Lake City: Deseret Book, 1988), 141–42.

"'Are You Having a Bad Day?'" by Mary Ellen Edmunds, from *Love Is a Verb* (Salt Lake City: Deseret Book, 1995), 3–4.

"Standing for Standards" by Randall C. Bird, from "Rad, Hot, Cool, and Awesome—Do Spirituality and Popularity Mix?" in *High Fives and High Hopes: Favorite Talks from Especially for Youth* (Salt Lake City: Deseret Book, 1990), 21–23.

Walking by Faith, I Am Blessed Every Hour

"Priceless Faith" by Hugh B. Brown, from Conference Report, October 1969, 106–7.

"Singing in the Choir" by Janice Kapp Perry, from "New Talents: Fun, Fear, and Fulfillment," in *May Christ Lift Thee Up: 1998 Women's Conference Talks* (Salt Lake City: Deseret Book, 1999), 244–45.

"The Ultimate Commitment" by Byron A. Rasmussen, in *Inspirational Missionary Stories,* comp. Leon Hartshorn (Salt Lake City: Deseret Book, 1976), 159–60.

"A Young Man's Awakening" by Kathryn Schlendorf, from "'Lord, I Believe, Help Thou Mine Unbelief,'" in *Living the Legacy* (Salt Lake City: Deseret Book, 1996), 204–6.

"A Mother's Prayer" by Teresa B. Clark. Previously unpublished.

"Laboring in the Trenches" by Carlfred Broderick, from "The Uses of Adversity," in *As Women of Faith: Talks Selected from the BYU Women's Conferences,* ed. Mary E. Stovall and Carol Cornwall Madsen (Salt Lake City: Deseret Book, 1989), 174–76.

"The Miracle of the Missing Notes" by Kim Novas, from "Hidden Pockets, Hidden Talents, and Profitable Servants," in *Living the Legacy* (Salt Lake City: Deseret Book, 1996), 76–78.

"'I Will Go! I Will Do It!'" by Heidi S. Swinton, from *Pioneer Spirit: Modern-Day Stories of Courage and Conviction* (Salt Lake City: Deseret Book, 1996), 74–75.

"A Letter Home" by Hugh B. Brown, from *The Abundant Life* (Salt Lake City: Bookcraft, 1965), 342–43.

"Invictus" by William Ernest Henley, in *Best-Loved Poems of the LDS People,* ed. Jack M. Lyon, Linda Ririe Gundry, Jay A. Parry, and Devan Jensen (Salt Lake City: Deseret Book, 1996), 42.

"The Soul's Captain: An Answer to 'Invictus'" by Orson F. Whitney, in *Best-Loved Poems of the LDS People,* ed. Jack M. Lyon, Linda Ririe Gundry, Jay A. Parry, and Devan Jensen (Salt Lake City: Deseret Book, 1996), 42–43.

"Beating the Enemy" by Heidi S. Swinton, from *Pioneer Spirit: Modern-Day Stories of Courage and Conviction* (Salt Lake City: Deseret Book, 1996), 72–73.

Do What Is Right

"Any Objections?" by Robert L. Simpson, from Conference Report, October 1963, 102.

"Mrs. America" by Vivian R. Cline, from "Integrity: What's Your Price?" in *Feeling Great, Hanging Tough, Doing Right* (Salt Lake City: Bookcraft, 1991), 118–24.

"Living the Truth" by Jack R. Christianson, from "Surviving the Teen Scene," in *High Fives and High Hopes* (Salt Lake City: Deseret Book, 1990), 46–49.

"God Make Me a Man" by Harlan Goldsbury Metcalf, in *Best-Loved Poems of the LDS People,* ed. Jack M. Lyon, Linda Ririe Gundry, Jay A. Parry, and Devan Jensen (Salt Lake City: Deseret Book, 1996), 45–46.

"Standing As a Daughter of God" by Leann P. Wheeler, from "Education: The Path that Leads Home," in *To Rejoice As Women: Talks from the 1994 Women's Conference,* ed. Susette Fletcher Green and Dawn Hall Anderson (Salt Lake City: Deseret Book, 1995), 235–37.

"'Get Behind Me, Satan!'" by John A. Widtsoe, from *In the Gospel Net: The Story of Anna Karine Gaarden Widtsoe* (Salt Lake City: Bookcraft, 1966), 73.

"A Glass of Lemonade" by David O. McKay, from *Cherished Experiences from the Writings of President David O. McKay,* rev. and enl., comp. Clare Middlemiss (Salt Lake City: Deseret Book, 1955), 199–200.

"A Life without Drugs" by Bill Stewart (a pseudonym), from Martha Nibley Beck and John C. Beck, *Breaking the Cycle of Compulsive Behavior* (Salt Lake City: Deseret Book, 1990), 245–48.

But a Small Moment

"Adversity" from William Shakespeare, *As You Like It,* 2.1.12–14.

"Into the Lion's Den" by William E. Berrett from *The Restored Church,* 7th ed. (Salt Lake City: Deseret Book, 1953), 229–32.

"Midnight in a Missouri Dungeon" by Parley P. Pratt, from *Autobiography of Parley P. Pratt* (Salt Lake City: Deseret Book, 1985), 179–80.

"'Life Has a Fair Number of Challenges in It'" by Eleanor Knowles, from *Howard W. Hunter* (Salt Lake City: Deseret Book, 1994), 304–6.

"A Life Well Lived" by Spencer W. Kimball, from "Integrity," in *BYU Speeches of the Year,* 25 February 1964, 7–8.

"I Keep Going One Day at a Time" by Anna Marie Perkins. Previously unpublished.

"Grateful for Pain? Never! Never?" by LaRene Gaunt. Previously unpublished.

"Crossing the Finish Line" by Art E. Berg, from "Some Miracles Take Time," in *Finding the Light in Deep Waters and Dark Times* (Salt Lake City: Bookcraft, 1992), 141–43.

"What God Hath Promised" by Annie Johnson Flint, in *Best-Loved Poems of the LDS People,* ed. Jack M. Lyon, Linda Ririe Gundry, Jay A. Parry, and Devan Jensen (Salt Lake City: Deseret Book, 1996), 1.

"Hope Despite Holocaust" by Lloyd D. Newell, from *The Divine Connection: Understanding Your Inherent Worth* (Salt Lake City: Deseret Book, 1992), 51–52.

The Integrity of the Heart

"A Daughter's Testimony" by Scott Anderson, from "Joseph Smith, the Restoration, and You," in *Joy in the Journey* (Salt Lake City: Deseret Book, 1998), 94–95.

"The Few" by Edgar A. Guest, in *Best-Loved Poems of the LDS People,* ed. Jack M. Lyon, Linda Ririe Gundry, Jay A. Parry, and Devan Jensen (Salt Lake City: Deseret Book, 1996), 1–2.

"A Trip to the Temple" by Mary Ellen Edmunds, from *Happiness: Finders, Keepers* (Salt Lake City: Deseret Book, 1999), 126–27.

"Elizabeth Francis Yates" by Chieko N. Okazaki, from *Lighten Up!* (Salt Lake City: Deseret Book, 1993), 58–59.

"'With Eyes Now Blazing'" by John A. Widtsoe, from *In the Gospel Net: The Story of Anna Karine Gaarden Widtsoe* (Salt Lake City: Bookcraft, 1966), 97–98.

"'I Must Join the Church'" by Marvin J. Ashton, from *Be of Good Cheer* (Salt Lake City: Deseret Book, 1987), 96.

"Inside the Front Cover" by Heidi S. Swinton, from *Pioneer Spirit: Modern-Day Stories of Courage and Conviction* (Salt Lake City: Deseret Book, 1996), 48–50.

"Prisoners No More" by Byung Sik Hong, in *Inspirational Missionary Stories,* comp. Leon Hartshorn (Salt Lake City: Deseret Book, 1976), 133–34.

"God Grant Me This" by Edgar A. Guest, in *Best-Loved Poems of the LDS People,* ed. Jack M. Lyon, Linda Ririe Gundry, Jay A. Parry, and Devan Jensen (Salt Lake City: Deseret Book, 1996), 163.

Fresh Courage Take . . . All Is Well

"'We Have Come Here to Kill Joe Smith'" by Lucy Mack Smith, from *History of Joseph Smith by His Mother* (Salt Lake City: Bookcraft, 1979), 254–56.

"And Thus History Was Made" by Nicholas G. Morgan, *Improvement Era,* July 1940, 399.

"Hole in the Rock" by Brent L. Top, from "It Still Takes Faith," in *Brigham Young University 1996–97 Speeches* (Provo: Brigham Young University, 1997), 336–37.

"Crossing the Sweetwater" by Solomon F. Kimball, from "Belated Emigrants of 1856," *Improvement Era,* February 1914, 287–88.

"'To Become Acquainted with God'" by David O. McKay, in *Relief Society Magazine,* January 1948, 8.

"The Journey of *Julia Ann*" by Karen Lynn Davidson, from "Shipboard Surprises and Shoreline Gleanings," in *Women and the Power Within: To See Life Steadily and See It Whole,* ed. Dawn Hall Anderson and Marie Cornwall (Salt Lake City: Deseret Book, 1991), 8–12.

"A Confirmation at the Water's Edge" by Priscilla Mogridge Staines, in *Remarkable Stories from the Lives of Latter-day Saint Women,* comp. Leon R. Hartshorn, 2 vols. (Salt Lake City: Deseret Book, 1973), 1:234–36.

"The Lost Oxen of Mary Fielding Smith" by Don C. Corbett, from *Mary Fielding Smith, Daughter of Britain: Portrait of Courage* (Salt Lake City: Deseret Book, 1966), 210–13.

"Healing the Oxen" by Don C. Corbett, from *Mary Fielding Smith, Daughter of Britain: Portrait of Courage* (Salt Lake City: Deseret Book, 1966), 228, 236–37.

"An Unexpected Visitor" by Clarissa Young Spencer,

from *Brigham Young at Home* (Salt Lake City: Deseret Book, 1961), 110.

God Our Strength Will Be

"The 'Shepard' Who Led Astray" by Kris Mackay, from *No Greater Love, and Other True Stories of Courage and Conviction* (Salt Lake City: Deseret Book, 1982), 53–58.

"Splits with Elder Begay" by Randal A. Wright, from "Learning for Myself," in *High Fives and High Hopes* (Salt Lake City: Deseret Book, 1990), 134–35.

"'This Is Where I Am Supposed to Be'" by Kathryn Schlendorf, from "'Lord, I Believe; Help Thou Mine Unbelief,'" in *Living the Legacy* (Salt Lake City: Deseret Book, 1996), 200–201.

"The Wrestling Champion of Niue Island" by Dean L. Thomson, in *Inspirational Missionary Stories,* comp. Leon Hartshorn (Salt Lake City: Deseret Book, 1976), 7–9.

"The Fruits of Faith" by Karl R. Koerner. Previously unpublished.

"'Why Do You Want to Go on This Mission, Son?'" by Harold B. Lee, from *Ye Are the Light of the World: Selected Sermons and Writings of Harold B. Lee* (Salt Lake City: Deseret Book, 1974), 111–12.

"The Courage of a Martyr" by Bryant S. Hinckley, from "The Youth and Early Manhood of Rudger Clawson," *Improvement Era,* March 1937, 135–37.

"The Men Were Masked" by John Alexander, in *Inspirational Missionary Stories,* comp. Leon Hartshorn (Salt Lake City: Deseret Book, 1976), 165–67.

"Returning Home" by Carlfred Broderick, from "The Uses of Adversity," in *As Women of Faith: Talks Selected from the BYU Women's Conferences,* ed. Mary E. Stovall and Carol Cornwall Madsen (Salt Lake City: Deseret Book, 1989), 178–81.

"'What If the Church Isn't True?'" by Robert L. Millet, from *Selected Writings of Robert L. Millet: Gospel Scholars Series* (Salt Lake City: Deseret Book, 2000), 368–69.

"Songs from the Heart," name withheld. Previously unpublished.

The Spirit Is Willing

"Joy for the 'Chemo' Queen" by Joanne Bair. Previously unpublished.

"The 'University of Disability'" by Marilynne Linford. Previously unpublished.

"'Please Don't Let Me Be Paralyzed'" by Donna Boss Linford. Previously unpublished.

"Alive and Still Kicking" by Kathy Ensign England. Previously unpublished.

"The Fighter" by S. E. Kiser, in *Best-Loved Poems of the American People* (Garden City, N.Y.: Garden City Books, 1936), 132–33.

"A Blessing in Disguise" by Marilynne Linford. Previously unpublished.

"Battling On" by Alison Horrocks Faifai. Previously unpublished.

"'There Are Many Things Worse than Cancer'" by Marilynne Linford. Previously unpublished.

"Who's in Charge?" by Carol Bernstrom Hogle. Previously unpublished.

"Bigger than the Mountain" by Carolyn M. Probst. Previously unpublished.

Thy Soldiers: Faithful, True, and Bold

"True Courage," author unknown, in *Best-Loved Poems of the LDS People,* ed. Jack M. Lyon, Linda Ririe Gundry, Jay A. Parry, and Devan Jensen (Salt Lake City: Deseret Book, 1996), 225.

"Sergeant Bulletproof" by Kris Mackay, from *Gift of Love* (Salt Lake City: Bookcraft, 1990), 48–51.

"St. Crispian's Day Speech" by William Shakespeare, from *King Henry V,* 4.3. 18–67.

"'Give Me Liberty or Give Me Death!'" by Patrick Henry.

"In Front of the Firing Squad" by Kris Mackay, from *No Greater Love, and Other True Stories of Courage and Conviction* (Salt Lake City: Deseret Book, 1982), 3–5.

"Loyalty and Honor in the 442nd" by Chieko N. Okazaki, from *Lighten Up!* (Salt Lake City: Deseret Book, 1993), 131–34.

"A Davao POW" by Richard Patterson. Previously unpublished.

"Opportunity" by Edward Rowland Sill, in *Best-Loved Poems of the LDS People,* ed. Jack M. Lyon, Linda Ririe Gundry, Jay A. Parry, and Devan Jensen (Salt Lake City: Deseret Book, 1996), 45.

"A Quiet Courage" by Franklin L. West, from Conference Report, April 1945, 116.

"A Million-Dollar Wound" by Chieko N. Okazaki, from *Lighten Up!* (Salt Lake City: Deseret Book, 1993), 134–36.

"The Source of a Convert's Courage" by Karl R. Koerner. Previously unpublished.

"'That Mad Englishwoman'" by Carol R. Gray, from

"Because I'm a Mother and I Love," in *May Christ Lift Thee Up: 1998 Women's Conference Talks* (Salt Lake City: Deseret Book, 1999), 146–49.

"Memorial Day" by Edgar A. Guest, in *Best-Loved Poems of the LDS People,* ed. Jack M. Lyon, Linda Ririe Gundry, Jay A. Parry, and Devan Jensen (Salt Lake City: Deseret Book, 1996), 214.

The Youth of Zion

"Proud to Be a Mormon" by Victor W. Harris, from "The Postcard Is for You!" in *Living the Legacy* (Salt Lake City: Deseret Book, 1996), 92.

"'A Great Teenage Girl'" by Margaret D. Nadauld, from *Write Back Soon!: Letters of Love and Encouragement to Young Women* (Salt Lake City: Deseret Book, 2001), 48–49.

"Courage in a Movie Theater Lobby" by Diane Bills Prince, from "Recognizing and Following the Spirit," in *Living the Legacy* (Salt Lake City: Deseret Book, 1996), 14–15.

"An Alternate Assignment" by Joan B. MacDonald, from *The Holiness of Everyday Life* (Salt Lake City: Deseret Book, 1995), 28–29.

"Before the Moment of Crisis" by Ed and Patricia Pinegar, from "Avoiding Temptation," in *Why Say No When the World Says Yes? Resisting Temptation in an Immoral World,* comp. Randal A. Wright (Salt Lake City: Deseret Book, 1993), 10–11.

"'She's a Mormon, and She Doesn't Drink'" by Barbara Lewis, from *Young Lions* (Salt Lake City: Deseret Book, 1993), 137–38.

"Helping Hands and Paws" by C. Tyler Briggs. Previously unpublished.

"Aimee Walker: An Olympic Hopeful" by Marilynne Linford. Previously unpublished.

"Saving a Friend" by Ardeth G. Kapp, from *I Walk by Faith* (Salt Lake City: Deseret Book, 1987), 141–45.